£1.50

PRESERVED STEAM
LOCOMOTIVES OF
WESTERN EUROPE
Volume 2

By the same author
On Railways at Home and Abroad
Locomotives Through the Lens
Men of the Footplate
On Engines in Britain and France
The Concise Encyclopaedia of World Railway Locomotives
(Editor and Contributor)
British Railways To-day
The Last Steam Locomotives of Western Europe
Die Letzten Dampflokomotiven Westeuropas
The World's Smallest Public Railway—RH & D
The Snowdon Mountain Railway
Last Steam Locomotives of British Railways
Southern Album
All About Photographing Trains
Ships and the Sea
The Royal Navy
Train Ferries of Western Europe
Eisenbahn-Fahren in Westeuropa

P. RANSOME-WALLIS

Preserved Steam
Locomotives of
Western Europe
Volume 2

LONDON

IAN ALLAN

First published 1971

SBN 7110 0210 X

Published by Ian Allan Ltd., Shepperton, Surrey and printed in the
United Kingdom by Tindal Press Ltd., London and Chelmsford

Contents

Acknowledgements   *page*   6

Introduction   8

Italy   11

    Narrow Gauge   40

Netherlands   45

    Narrow Gauge   61

Norway   63

    Narrow Gauge   76

Portugal   85

Spain   91

    Narrow Gauge   133

Sweden   139

    Narrow Gauge   171

Switzerland   215

    Narrow Gauge   248

Appendix 1: Locomotive Manufacturers 267

Appendix 2: Location of Preserved
    and Stored Locomotives   271

Appendix 3: Alterations and additions
    to December 31, 1970   279

Bibliography   285

Acknowledgements

In the compilation of this book I have been greatly helped by many people in many ways. I am indebted to them all and I offer to them my sincere thanks.

Austria: Dipl. Ing. Rolf Niederhuemer, Technical Museum, Vienna.

Belgium: AMUTRA, Secretary and Members, Schepdael; Monsieur A. Vanden Eede, SNCV, Brussels; Director General SNCB, Brussels; Edgar T. Mead, Jnr., Steamtown, Bellows Falls, USA.

Denmark: W. E. Danker-Jensen, Esq., Railway Museum, Copenhagen; O. Winther Laursen, Esq., Kölding.

Finland: Igor Ahvenlahti, Esq., VR. Helsinki.

France: Monsieur Michel Doerr, Director of Railway Museum, Mulhouse; Herr A. W. Glaser, Zürich, Switzerland; N. A. Needle, Esq., London, England; J. A. Price, Esq., London, England; Monsieur C. Roche, SNCF, Paris.

West Germany: Dr. Ing. Glaser, Bundesbahndirektion, Frankfurt; Dr. Joachim Hotz, DEGB, Karlsruhe; Dr. Pfahl, Verkehrsmuseum, Nüremberg; Herr Wolfgang Stoffels, Augsburg; Charles Walker, Esq., Hildenborough, England.

Italy: P. M. Kalla-Bishop, Esq., London, England; Sr. Carlo Saura, Leonardo da Vinci Museum, Milan.

Netherlands: Miss Marie-Anne Asselberghs, Director, Railway Museum, Utrecht; N.V. Machinefabrik, Breda; Robert Stamkot, Esq., Stichting Museum, Buurtspoorweg, Enschede.

Norway: "E.F." of the Public Relations Dept. NSB, Oslo.

Portugal: Senor Antonio Gouveia, C.P., Lisbon.

Spain: Don Senor Antonio Lago Carbello, RENFE, Madrid; Lawrence Marshall, Esq., Crawley, England; Don Señor Gustavo Reder, Madrid.

Sweden: C. A. Alrenius, Esq., SJ, Stockholm; Ulf Diehl, Esq., Lidingo; G. Ekeroth, Esq., SJ, Stockholm; L. O. Karlsson, Esq., Sollentuna; Rolf Larsson, Esq., Göteborg; Trygve Romsloe, Esq., Narvik, Norway; Erik Sundström, Esq., Karlskoga.

Switzerland: B.L.S. Publicity Department, Bern; Manfred Meier, Esq., Mettmenstetten; Herr Fr. Neuenschwander, EBT, Burgdorf; Renfer et Cie, Bienne; Herr W. Trüb, SBB, Bern; Von Moos 'schon AG; Von Roll AG, Gerlafingen; Herr Hans Wismann, Verkehrshaus, Lucerne.

The following have provided much help and information about locomotives in several countries and my thanks go to: B. M. Campbell, Esq.; D. Cole, Esq.; J. Eberstein, Esq.; R. S. Fraser, Esq.; Brian Garvin, Esq.; A. G. W. Goff, Esq.; A. J. Hart, Esq.; J. H. Price, Esq.; F. L. Pugh, Esq.; D. F. Rollins, Esq.; Trevor Rowe, Esq.; Brian Stephenson, Esq.

My old and valued friends Othmar Bamer of Vienna, Austria and Maurice Maillet of Lagny, France have once again uncomplainingly and generously given me all the support and help for which I asked. I am most grateful.

Finally, without the able assistance and information so generously given by R. G. ("Tommy") Farr, this book could never have been written. Once upon a time I thought I knew quite a lot about continental locomotives. "Tommy" Farr begins where I leave off! I can only again say "Thank you".

Photographs

The photographs in this book have come from many sources and each is acknowledged with the caption. My sincere thanks to all those who have helped in this way.

P. R-W.

Introduction

In Western Continental Europe, as in other parts of the world, the interest in the preservation of steam railway locomotives is growing apace. Rather belatedly, the various railways have begun to recognise this interest and many are now showing concern to secure for posterity representative examples of their individual steam locomotive practice.

Two major problems are common to all who try to preserve locomotives: To find adequate money to do so and to find suitable and adequate space for the purpose. Many praiseworthy efforts, both private and public, have foundered on the failure to obtain one or both of these requirements. In other cases, preservation of large tender locomotives has proved difficult to achieve and has been abandoned in favour of keeping some small and mechanically uninteresting tank locomotives.

It is the avowed intention of most countries to establish, at least one, railway museum, but the locations have not all been finalised and the space to be available for locomotives is, therefore, not known. As a result, a considerable number of locomotives which have been withdrawn from service is to be found in the sheds, yards and depots of most Western European countries. Some of these will, undoubtedly, find their ultimate homes in museums or as monuments. Others will go for scrap but which will survive has often not yet been decided. Frequent changes occur also, as more "candidates for preservation" arrive, their active lives completed.

In this book, I have had five objectives:

(1) To describe technically and historically, as far as possible, all those Continental Western European standard and broad-gauge steam locomotives which have been preserved and those which are stored for probable future preservation. I fully realise that some which are described will probably end their days as scrap metal rather than in a museum but, until the final decision has been made as to which they are to be, I have thought it better to include, rather than to neglect them. There may be some I have omitted, owing to my ignorance of their existence, but I do not think these are many. In the descriptions in this book, however, only *complete* locomotives are dealt with and the many interesting locomotive parts which are to be found in museums and technical schools have not been included.

(2) To provide as much information as possible about preserved steam locomotives from narrow gauge railways (1067 mm and less). The situation concerning these locomotives is still very fluid. In this book, an

account is given of those locomotives which are known to be preserved or which are at work on "museum railways". The roster is by no means complete and neither is the technical and historical information available.

(3) To illustrate all the classes of locomotives described. I realise that this is the most important feature of the book but it has not been easy to achieve. However, for the standard and broad gauge, only in a few instances has it been impossible. Narrow gauge locomotives have proved to be much more difficult and many recorded are, unfortunately, not illustrated. No attempt is made always to show the actual preserved locomotive. A good picture of a machine of the same type and class is preferable to showing a view of the half-dismembered remains of the actual engine "stored for restoration and preservation".

(4) To afford the reader easy identification of the locomotives described. The current running number and, wherever relevant, the previous running number(s) are given. In most cases it has been possible to provide details of the builder, works number and date of construction.

(5) To give leading dimensions of each locomotive. Here, consideration of space resulted in the decision to record only cylinder diameter and stroke, coupled (or driving) wheel diameter, grate area and boiler pressure. Again, narrow gauge locomotive records are very incomplete.

The scope of this work *does NOT include industrial locomotives* which are preserved. An exception is made, however, in describing *SOME* of those which are actually working on narrow-gauge "museum railways".

The compilation of this book became something of a major research project, complicated by the inevitable author's nightmare that frequently no two "reliable" sources of information were in agreement. I am always grateful to those who write to me offering constructive criticism and informed correction.

As a result of two World Wars, many locomotives were sent away from their railways of origin and spent most of their lives on the railways of other countries. These permanent transfers were mostly of German locomotives, though many engines of Austrian origin were also to be found "away from home". In this book, all such locomotives which are preserved are included in the lists of their countries of origin. The same plan has been followed to include locomotives built away from the country of their original design. Thus, German Series 42, built in

Austria and sold to Luxembourg, is included in Germany though preserved in Luxembourg.

Finally, a word about the locations given for stored locomotives. These are in accordance with the best information available at this time. Movements of such locomotives from one depot to another are commonplace, so it is unwise to regard all the locations given as permanent. Most railways do not allow visits to depots solely occupied by locomotives in store as a regrettably large number of thefts of number plates etc., have occurred when such facilities have been made available in the past. However, it is probable that many stored locomotives may be exhibited, on a rota basis, in the museums. This principle has already been adopted in Switzerland where the locomotives in store at Vallorbe are brought, four at a time, to the Verkehrshaus at Lucerne for six-monthly periods of exhibition. Thus there is an added incentive for students of locomotive history to visit the museum each year.

December 1970   P. R-W.

Note regarding Boiler Pressures

There are differences between railways in the units used to express boiler pressures.

Those in general use on European Railways are:

(i) Kilograms per Square Centimetre (kg/cm²)
$$1 \text{ kg/cm}^2 = 14 \cdot 2 \text{ pounds per square inch (p.s.i.)}$$
(ii) Atmosphere (atm)
$$1 \text{ atm} = 1 \cdot 03 \text{ kg/cm}^2 = 14 \cdot 7 \text{ p.s.i.}$$
(iii) Hectopiezes (hpz)
$$1 \text{ hpz} = 1 \cdot 02 \text{ kg/cm}^2 = 14 \cdot 5 \text{ p.s.i.}$$

For all *practical* purposes these units may be regarded as equivalents.

Italian State Railways

The Italian State Railways, *Ferrovie Dello Stato*—FS, was formed in 1905 by the nationalisation of three large private companies. These companies were *Rete Adriatica*, *Rete Mediterraneo* and the *Rete Sicule*. Originally the railways used steam traction but Italy was among the first countries to experiment with electric traction and, to-day, nearly 50 per cent of the lines are electrified. The remainder are operated almost entirely by diesel-electric power.

Steam Locomotives and their Preservation in Italy

The principal collection of preserved steam locomotives in Italy is in Milan at the Leonardo da Vinci Museum of Science and Technology in the Via San Vittore. This museum at present houses 14 1435mm-gauge and two narrow-gauge steam locomotives. These exhibits which were formerly in the small FS Museum at Rome Termini Station have been transferred to Milan.

Outside the museum there is a number of locomotives in store at Rome, Smistamento Depot and at Turin Motive Power Depot and these are to be preserved and put on display as and when suitable space becomes available.

Apart from the official railway preservation plans there is little of note in Italy. Two small locomotives are kept in public parks and two others are preserved privately.

Italy has always been very short of coal, and until the enforcing of sanctions against her in 1936, relied largely on supplies from Britain, especially of steam coal from South Wales.

Locomotive design often reflected the need for coal economy, and compound locomotives of several types were built, but were finally rejected or converted to simple. Several examples of the Plancher four-cylinder compound 0–10–0s, however, remained in service until recent years and one has been preserved (page 22).

No steam locomotive development occurred in Italy after 1930 but some outstanding modifications were made to existing types, and were adopted in the designs of many locomotives all over the world.

Poppet valves of the Caprotti type, which were first applied to an FS locomotive in 1921, were the idea of an Italian motor engineer and were successful, particularly in modified form, greatly improving the steam distribution and therefore the economy of FS locomotives.

Undoubtedly the most controversial of all fuel economy measures adopted in 1937 by the Italian Railways was the Franco-Crosti boiler, in which the flue gases and exhaust steam are led back from the smokebox through two economisers, to exhaust from two laterally placed chimneys in front of the cab. A modified form with a single economiser (the Crosti boiler) was used for the FS 2–8–0s of Group 741. The final low temperature and lowered velocity of the smokebox gases at exhaust allowed the formation of sulphuric acid which caused severe corrosion of economiser tubes and other parts of the system. The Italians always claimed that they suffered only slightly from this trouble and that it occurred mostly at the chimney top, a claim which was in turn, doubted and explained by the use on the FS of British coal with a very low sulphur content. Chrome steel was, however, used for the chimneys of some Crosti engines. It seems a glaring and curious omission that none of these interesting locomotives has been preserved or is scheduled for preservation.

Many Italian locomotive designs included the Zara, or Italian truck in which the leading radial wheels and the leading coupled wheels form a bogie and are mounted in a separate frame which is pivoted in such a manner as to allow most side-play in the radial wheels and less in the leading coupled wheels. Engines to which this truck was fitted included all 2–6–0, 2–6–2, 2–8–0 and 2–10–0 types and their tank engine equivalents, except those of foreign origin.

Apart from main lines most of the routes of the FS are laid with comparatively light rail and $16\frac{1}{2}$ tonnes was the maximum axle load for general purpose steam locomotives. Only on a small number of main line locomotives was this limit exceeded. In order to get maximum power for minimum axle loading, a number of locomotives was built with the lightest possible plate frames and with inside cylinders having piston valves outside the frames. There were 2–6–0s and 2–8–0 mixed traffic engines with this arrangement.

The largest Italian passenger locomotives were the four-cylinder Pacifics of Group 691 and the largest freight engines were 18 two-cylinder simple 2–10–0s of Group 480 designed for the Brenner line. Neither was outstanding by modern standards. Although the first European 4–8–0 appeared in Italy in 1902, no engines of this wheel arrangement have been preserved.

Detail of BAYARD in the Leonardo da Vinci Museum at Milan. The general appearance of the locomotive is almost identical with that of the Netherlands DE AREND (page 47)   [FS

The first steam locomotive in Italy was a 2–2–2 with two inside cylinders, built for the *Ferrovia Napoli-Portici* by Longridge and Company of Newcastle-upon-Tyne, England in 1839 and it was their works number 120. It was named *BAYARD* and hauled the first train from Naples to Portici on October 3, 1839. This locomotive was almost identical with that built for the broader-gauge Amsterdam-Haarlem Railway in Holland which was Longridge No 119.

A full-size working replica of this locomotive was built for the Centenary Celebrations of Italian Railways in 1939 by the Railway Workshops at Turin. It was first placed on display in the museum at Rome Termini but is now on exhibition in the Museum of Science and Technology, Milan.

Dimensions: CYLINDERS: 355 × 425mm

                 DRIVING WHEELS: 1702mm

                 BOILER PRESSURE: 3.5kg/cm^2

No 552.036 in the Museum at Milan   [FS

No 552.036 was built in 1900 by Breda (works number 479) as No 1900 for the Adriatic Railway (*Rete Adriatica*) on which it was Group 180. Thirty-six of the Group were built and they had horizontal outside cylinders with inside Stephenson link motion operating slide valves inside the frames. Round-top boilers and a generous cab contributed to the handsome appearance of these engines. Considering the numerous gradients of the routes over which they worked, the coupled wheels, 1920mm in diameter, were comparatively large but their maximum allowed speed was only 95km/h.

Thirteen of these engines survived in service until after the end of World War II. No 552.036 is now on exhibition in the Museum of Science and Technology at Milan.

Dimensions: CYLINDERS: 480 × 600mm
COUPLED WHEELS: 1920mm
GRATE AREA: 2.3m^2
BOILER PRESSURE: 10kg/cm^2

ITALY   0–6–0   1435mm

No 290.319 is an outside-cylinder 0–6–0 freight locomotive with inside Stephenson link motion. It is the survivor of 338 locomotives which were built between 1899 and 1912 having been introduced as Group 350 of the Adriatic Railway (*Rete Adriatica*) and others built for FS after 1906 as Group 290.
They had the usual Italian arrangement of two safety valves, Coale valves over the firebox and a Salter valve on the dome. They had nearly all been withdrawn from service by the end of World War II.

No 290.319 was built in 1912 by *Officine Meccaniche Milan* (OM) and was their works number 489. It is in store at Rome Smistamento Depot for future preservation.

Dimensions: CYLINDERS: 455 × 650mm
                COUPLED WHEELS: 1510mm
                GRATE AREA: 2.0m²
                BOILER PRESSURE: 12kg/cm²

2–6–0 No 640.146 of the same class as the preserved locomotive [P. Ransome-Wallis]

No 640.106 was originally FS No 64106 and is a superheated 2–6–0 passenger locomotive which was built in 1910 by Breda (works number 1188). It is at Rome, Smistamento Depot, in store for future preservation and display.

 The 2–6–0 type was well suited to the many secondary lines of the FS which were sharply curved and laid with light rail. There were several groups of them and the antecedents of the 173 engines of Group 640* introduced in 1907 were two-cylinder non-superheated compounds of Group 630 introduced in 1905, some of which were later rebuilt as superheated simples to Group 640.3xx.

 Group 640 have inside cylinders with outside piston valves driven by Walschaerts valve gear. Several engines of the group were later rebuilt with rotary cam Caprotti valves. The leading radial axle forms an Italian truck with the leading coupled axle.

Dimensions: CYLINDERS: 540 × 700mm
     COUPLED WHEELS: 1850mm
     GRATE AREA: 2.4m²
     BOILER PRESSURE: 12kg/cm²
     SUPERHEATED

* *Four of these were built for the Santhia Biella Railway and were later FS 640.170–173.*

No 680.037 was built in 1907 by Breda (works number 854). It is now stored at Rome, Smistamento Depot awaiting preservation.

The express passenger 2–6–2 locomotives of Group 680 were introduced in 1906. They were Plancher four-cylinder balanced compounds, the two high pressure cylinders with a common piston valve being on the Right-hand side of the engine and the two low pressure cylinders, also with a common piston valve, on the Left-hand side. They had Walschaerts valve gear and were not superheated. The two leading axles of the engine were combined in an Italian truck.

From 1910 some of the engines of Group 680 were superheated and the boiler pressure reduced to 14 kg/cm². These engines formed Group 681. From 1922 some engines of both Groups were given new and larger high pressure cylinders and, where necessary, superheaters and these became Group 682.

Dimensions: CYLINDERS: HIGH PRESSURE: 360 × 650mm
                 LOW PRESSURE: 590 × 650mm
      COUPLED WHEELS: 850mm
      GRATE AREA: 3.5m²
      BOILER PRESSURE: 16kg/cm²

No s685.558 is a locomotive of the same class and ancestry as No s685.600 [P. R-W

No s685.600 is preserved and is on exhibition at the Museum of Science and Technology at Milan. It was built as a Plancher four-cylinder compound 2–6–2 in 1908 by Breda (works number 1000) and was originally numbered 6900. It then became No 68100 and finally, while still in its original form, 680.100 (see Group 680). It was rebuilt in 1934 as a four-cylinder simple engine with rotary-cam Caprotti valves.

Group 685, four-cylinder 2–6–2 express locomotives were introduced in 1912 and 241 were built. The four high pressure cylinders were in line and there was a common piston valve to each pair of cylinders. Another 30 were built with Caprotti valves in 1926 and five of these were rebuilt with Franco-Crosti boilers and given streamlined casings in 1939–41. Four of the earlier engines of Group 685 were rebuilt with Caprotti valves but all retained the boiler pressure of 12kg/cm².

From 1925, many of the old compound engines of Groups 680, 681 and 682 (qv) were rebuilt as Group 685 with four high pressure cylinders and superheaters and some were later again rebuilt with Caprotti valves. In all these the boiler pressure was 12kg/cm².

From 1930 many more of these old compounds were rebuilt as superheated four-cylinder simples but they had boiler pressure 16kg/cm², trefoil blast pipes with wide chimneys, Knorr feed-water pumps and heaters and all had Caprotti valves. They were numbered in the s685.502–651 series and it is from this Group that the museum exhibit, No s685.600, is taken.

Dimensions: CYLINDERS (4): 420 × 650mm

         COUPLED WHEELS: 1850mm

         GRATE AREA: 3.5m²

         BOILER PRESSURE: 16kg/cm²

         SUPERHEATED

No 691.027 is a four-cylinder 4–6–2 of the same class as the preserved locomotive   [P. R-W

No 691.022 was built in 1914 by Breda (works number 1471) as FS No 69022 and which later became No 690.022. It is now exhibited in the Museum of Science and Technology in Milan.

    Group 691 consisted of 33 four-cylinder 4–6–2 locomotives which were 1928–33 rebuilds of the 33 four-cylinder 4–6–2s built 1911–14 by Breda, OM and Ansaldo. The rebuilding was largely concerned with the provision of better designed and larger boilers which were interchangeable with those of the 2–8–2s of Group 746 (qv).

    The four cylinders had common piston valves for each pair and all drove the middle coupled axle. The sandbox was located around the steam dome, a usual feature of later Italian steam locomotive practice. They were limited by their 19-tonne axle-load to a few main lines, eg Venice-Rome, Udine-Venice. Despite their considerable power, they were disappointingly sluggish machines with poorly designed short-travel piston valves.

Dimensions: CYLINDERS (4): 450 × 680mm
            COUPLED WHEELS: 2050mm
            GRATE AREA: 4.3m²
            BOILER PRESSURE: 14kg/cm²
            SUPERHEATED

No 736.226 is identical with the preserved locomotive   [P. R-W

No 736.202 was No 3693 of the United States Army Transportation Corps and was built in 1944 by Lima (works number 8606). It is stored at Rome, Smistamento Depot and will be preserved.

Some 1,897 of these rugged bar-framed 2–8–0 locomotives were built to the design of Major J. W. Marsh of the US Army Corps of Engineers by the American Locomotive Company (ALCO), Baldwin Locomotive Company and Lima Locomotive Company for the United States Army Transportation Corps. After serving the Armies behind the Western Front, in North Africa and in Italy, 243 of them were left with FS who were then desperately in need of railway motive power. These 2–8–0s were among the best locomotives ever to work in Italy but were unpopular as there were several instances of their firebox crown plates collapsing with dire results.

Dimensions: CYLINDERS: 483 × 660mm
                COUPLED WHEELS: 1478mm
                GRATE AREA: 3.8m²
                BOILER PRESSURE: 15.8kg/cm²
                SUPERHEATED

No 746.034 is a four-cylinder compound 2-8-2 of the same class as the preserved locomotive [P. R-W

No 746.031 is a four-cylinder compound 2–8–2 built in 1922 by Breda (works number 2003). It is preserved and exhibited at the Museum of Science and Technology at Milan.

Fifty of these large engines were built in 1922. The high pressure cylinders were inside the frames and the low pressure outside; all drove the third coupled axle. Each set of (outside) Walschaerts valve gear drove one high pressure and one low pressure piston valve, the drive for the former being taken off the combination lever on each side. The valves were set so that the low pressure cut-off was always 12–15 per cent greater than that of the high pressure valve.

In 1926 a further ten locomotives of Group 746 were built with rotary cam Caprotti valves.

An axle loading of only 16½ tonnes gave these big compounds a wide range of availability, but they were indifferent performers and most of them ended their days, out of service, in Sicily.

Dimensions: CYLINDERS: HIGH PRESSURE: 490 × 680mm
                                    LOW PRESSURE: 720 × 680mm
COUPLED WHEELS: 1880mm
GRATE AREA: 4.3m^2
BOILER PRESSURE: 14kg/cm^2
SUPERHEATED

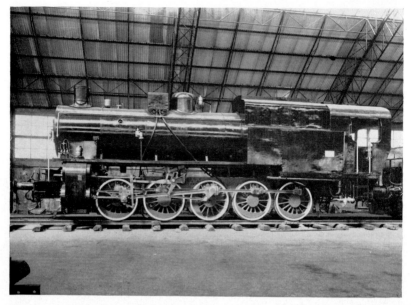

No 470.092 in the Leonardo da Vinci Museum of Science and Technology at Milan. The coal bunker over the left-hand side of the firebox is clearly seen   [FS

No 470.092 is a four-cylinder compound 0–10–0 locomotive which was originally No 4792 and was built in 1908 by *Officine Meccaniche Milan* (works number 241). It is preserved and on display at the Museum of Science and Technology in Milan.

One hundred and forty-three of these four-cylinder Plancher compound 0–10–0 locomotives were built between 1907 and 1911, the first 12 and some others by Maffei and the remainder by Italian builders. The two high pressure cylinders (one inside and one outside the frames), with their common piston valves, were on the Right hand side of the engine and the two similarly disposed low pressure cylinders were on the Left hand side. The cut-off could be combined or independent by the engagement or dis-engagement of two toothed wheels on the reverser in the cab. Group 470 were built without superheaters but later engines were superheated and were Group 471 which also included earlier engines which were subsequently superheated.

These locomotives were designed for working freight trains on heavily graded mountain lines and also they were extensively used for banking. They were built with an enclosed cab and with a four-wheeled tender which carried 13m³ of water and had a cabin at the rear end for the *chef de train*. Four tonnes of coal was carried in a bunker situated on the Left hand side and on top of the rear end of the boiler and, later, coal rails were added to the tender tank-top so that an extra 1.6 tonnes could be carried thereon.

A number of these engines were later rebuilt with open ended cabs and conventional six-wheeled tenders. The coal bunkers were then removed from the boiler tops. Some of these converted engines were working in Sicily until 1966 in the train ferry yards at Messina.

Dimensions: CYLINDERS: HIGH PRESSURE: 375 × 650mm

LOW PRESSURE: 610 × 650mm

COUPLED WHEELS: 1360mm

GRATE AREA: 3.5m²

BOILER PRESSURE: 16kg/cm²

No BG 34 TREZZO   [D. Trevor Rowe

No BG 34 *TREZZO* is an inside-cylinder 0–4–0 Tram locomotive with solid wheels and a horizontal locomotive type boiler. It was built in 1909 by Henschel (works number 9716) for working on the Milan-Gallarate Tramway. This line, which extends some 44km north-westwards from Milan, was completely electrified by the end of 1952 at which time No BG 34 was sold to the Monza-Trezzo-Bergamo Tramway which extended 23km from Monza to Bergamo. This line, which gave the engine its name, was closed in 1958, though the Trezzo Bergamo section had closed in 1952 because of the weakness of a bridge at Trezzo.

No BG 34 was sent to Rome, Smistamento Depot and has now been put on display in the Museum of Science and Technology at Milan.
Dimensions: NOT KNOWN

No 111 is an inside cylinder 0–4–0 Tram locomotive with solid wheels and a locomotive type boiler. It is very similar to the previously described locomotive No BG 34 and it has been sectioned and is exhibited in the Tramways Section of the Museum of Science and Technology in Milan.

It was built in 1912 by Tubize (works number 1683) for the Milan-Pavia Tramway which extended 31km almost due west from Milan.

In 1935 No 111 was sold to the Milan-Magenta Tramway which extended about 110km due south from Milan to Pavia but which ceased operating towards the end of World War II.

Dimensions: NOT KNOWN

No 800.008 as preserved   [P. R-W

No 800.008 is an 0–4–0 Back Tank locomotive with two outside cylinders, Walschaerts valve gear and a vertical boiler. It was constructed as an 0–4–2 baggage car No 663 in 1907 by Maffei (works number 2656) rebuilt in 1913, and is at present stored at Turin Motive Power Depot.

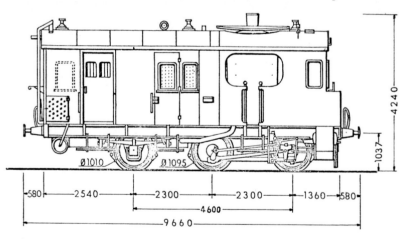

This drawing shows No 800.008 before re-building   [FSO

Seventeen of these powered baggage cars (*Automotrice a Vapore*) were built in 1907–08 but their usefulness seems to have been over-rated and, from 1912 onwards, the baggage compartment with its supporting axle was cut away and of the motive power ends, some became 0–4–0T shunting engines and others train heating boilers.

No 800.008 was, for many years, shed pilot at Turin and was a distinctly powerful and lively unit for its size.

Dimensions: CYLINDERS: 290 × 400mm

COUPLED WHEELS: 1095mm

BOILER PRESSURE: 13kg/cm²

4–4–0T No 22

[P. M. Kalla-Bishop Collection

No 22, a 4–4–0 Side Tank locomotive of the Monza-Molteno-Oggiono Railway (since 1954 part of the FS) was built as No 254 *LUINO* for the Nord Milan Railway in 1896 by Couillet (works number 1148). The Nord Milan sold it in 1930 when their suburban services were completely electrified.

With piston valves operated by outside Walschaerts gear and a Belpaire boiler, this little engine was a fine example of contemporary Belgian locomotive design and construction. It has been in store since 1954 at Rome, Smistamento Depot, and is scheduled for preservation.
Dimensions: NOT KNOWN

ITALY 0–6–0T 1435mm

Privately preserved on an estate near Turin is an outside-cylinder 0–6–0T
which was built as No 6801 *GARIGLIANTE* for the Mediterranean
Railway (*Rete Mediterraneo*) in 1900 by Costruzioni Meccaniche Saronno
(works number 127).
This locomotive became FS 8291 in 1906.
Dimensions: NOT KNOWN

No 830.021 is of the same class as No 830.035   [P. R-W

No 830.035 was originally FS No 8335 and is an outside-cylinder 0–6–0
Side Tank locomotive which was built in 1906 by Breda (works number
776). It is stored at Rome, Smistamento Depot, for future preservation
and display.

These engines were introduced in 1903 by the Mediterranean Railway
(*Rete Mediterraneo*) and the FS continued to build them after 1905. Some
of them were still at work in Genoa Docks until 1969.
Dimensions: CYLINDERS: 380 × 580mm
        COUPLED WHEELS: 1310mm
        GRATE AREA: 1.4m²
        BOILER PRESSURE: 12 kg/cm²

No 835.185 which is identical with the preserved locomotive [P. R-W

No 835.186 was originally FS No 83686 and it was built in 1910 by Officine Meccaniche, Milan (works number 322). It is preserved and is exhibited at the Museum of Science and Technology, Milan.

Locomotives of Group 835 were the standard shunting 0–6–0 Side Tank locomotives of the FS. They were introduced in 1906 and 370 were built, being familiarly known as the "coffee pots". When the boilers of some of them wore out, the frames and running gear were in such excellent condition that they were used for reconstruction into DC electric shunting locomotives of Group E 321.

Dimensions: CYLINDERS: 410 × 580mm
COUPLED WHEELS: 1310mm
GRATE AREA: 1.4m^2
BOILER PRESSURE: 12kg/cm^2

Smokebox detail of NORD 0–6–0WT No 250.05 in the Museum at Milan [FS

Nord Milan No 250.05 is on exhibition in the Museum of Science and Technology, Milan. It was built in 1915 by Costruzioni Meccaniche Saronno (works number 548) but, in the museum, it carries, in error, the maker's plate of Esslingen 2163/86.

This locomotive was one of six 0–6–0 Well Tank shunting locomotives built for the Nord Milan between 1887 and 1917 with round-top boilers

31

and outside cylinders with slide valves operated by outside Stephenson link motion.

Dimensions: CYLINDERS: 400 × 510mm
COUPLED WHEELS: 1275mm
GRATE AREA: 1.4m²
BOILER PRESSURE: 10kg/cm²

0–6–0T No 1 of the SNFT

[Lance King

Preserved and on display in the Castle Park at Brescia is No 1, an outside-cylinder 0–6–0 Side Tank locomotive with outside Allan link motion built in 1906 by Esslingen (works number 3392) for the *Società Nazionale Ferrovie e Tranvie*. This company operates two lines with a total of 98km, the first between Iseo and Rovato and the second, for which No 1 was built, linking Brescia-Iseo and Edola. The lines are now operated by diesel traction.

Dimensions: NOT KNOWN

SATTI No 9   [P. M. Kalla-Bishop Collection

Preserved and on display in a park at Loano, 30km from Savona, is outside-cylinder 0–6–0 Well Tank locomotive No 9 of the *S.p.Az. Torinese Tranvie Intercomunal* (SATTI). This locomotive was built in 1907 by Henschel (works number 7329). It has slide valves operated by Allan link motion.

Dimensions: NOT KNOWN

2–6–oT No 905.032   [D. Trevor Rowe

No 905.032 was originally FS No 90532 built in 1910 by Breda (works number 1226) and it is stored at Rome, Smistamento Depot, awaiting preservation.

It is a 2–6–0 Well Tank locomotive, one of 84 introduced in 1908 for service on steeply-graded mountain secondary lines. They were smart little engines with Walschaerts valve gear operating piston valves but they were not superheated.

Dimensions: CYLINDERS: 455 × 700mm
             COUPLED WHEELS: 1360mm
             GRATE AREA: 1.6m²
             BOILER PRESSURE: 12kg/cm²

No 880.159 was originally FS No 87559 and then 875.059. It was built in 1914 by Breda (works number 1512) and it is preserved and on display in the Museum of Science and Technology at Milan.

Group 875 consisted of 117 2–6–0 Side Tank locomotives introduced in 1912. They had cylinders 390mm in diameter with slide valves operated by Walschaerts valve gear and were without superheaters. In 1915

34

No 880.175 is a 2–6–0 T identical with the preserved locomotive [P. R-W

locomotives of Group 880 were introduced and 60 were built. They had superheaters and piston valves with cylinders 450mm diameter. In all other respects they were identical with Group 875.

From 1920 onwards, a number of engines of Group 875 were rebuilt as Group 880 and numbered in the 880.100 and 880.200 series. They could easily be distinguished from the original engines of Group 880 by their wider outside steam-pipe covers. The preserved locomotive is one of these rebuilds.

Dimensions: CYLINDERS: 450 × 580mm
COUPLED WHEELS: 1510mm
GRATE AREA: 1.5m^2
BOILER PRESSURE: 12kg/cm^2
SUPERHEATED

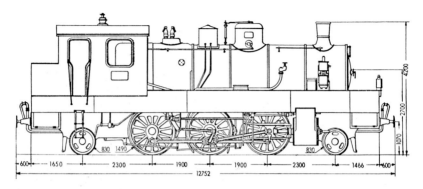

Outlined drawing showing a 2–6–2T of Series 910   [FS

No 910.001 was built in 1905 as No 401 for the Sicilian Railways (*Rete Sicule*) by Ansaldo (works number 487). This is the first of 54 two-cylinder compound 2–6–2 Well Tank locomotives which were originally built for Sicily but six of them later were used on the Milan suburban services. No 910.001 is in store at Rome, Smistamento Depot and is to be preserved.

These locomotives were without superheaters. The cylinders were outside the frames, the high pressure being on the Left-hand side of the engine and the low pressure on the Right. Steam distribution was by a piston valve for the high pressure and a slide valve for the low pressure cylinder. The layout of the Walschaerts valve gear was unusual in that the eccentric rod from the return crank was taken *backwards* to the expansion link which was at the level of the leading edge of the rear coupled wheel. This necessitated a very long radius rod and gave the engines a peculiar "cross legged" appearance when running (cf. *LANGNAU*, page 228).

Dimensions: CYLINDERS: HIGH PRESSURE: 460 × 600mm
LOW PRESSURE: 700 × 600mm
COUPLED WHEELS: 1490mm
GRATE AREA: 2.4m²
BOILER PRESSURE: 13kg/cm²

0–8–0WT No 895.159 of the same Group as No 895.028. This photograph shows the additional coal bunker in front of the cab which was fitted to some of these engines   [P. R-W

No 895.028 is an 0–8–0 Well Tank locomotive which is preserved in a pinewood at Marina di Pietrasanta on the main line between Pisa and La Spezia.

One hundred and seven of these heavy shunting locomotives of Group 895 were built between 1908 and 1915 by Henschel and by Italian builders. They had two connected but separate well tanks placed above the frames and below the running plates. Walschaerts valve gear drove slide valves above the two outside cylinders and the trailing axle had 40mm movement each side of centre.

In 1921 another series of similar engines was introduced. These had superheaters, piston valves and slightly larger cylinders. They were Group 896.

Dimensions: (of Group 895):
       CYLINDERS: 530 × 520mm
       COUPLED WHEELS: 1095mm
       GRATE AREA: 1.63m^2
       BOILER PRESSURE: 12kg/cm^2

No 940.006 is identical with the preserved locomotive   [P. R-W

No 940.001 was built in 1921 by Officine Meccaniche, Milan (works number 795) and is preserved and exhibited at the Museum of Science and Technology, Milan. It is a powerful superheated 2–8–2 Side Tank locomotive for freight duties on mountain lines.

Fifty-three locomotives of Group 940 were built, three of which were built originally for the Santhia-Biella Railway. They were the tank-engine version of the 2–8–0s of Group 740, a straightforward, uncomplicated design. Some are still at work (1970).

Dimensions: CYLINDERS: 540 × 700mm

COUPLED WHEELS: 1370mm

GRATE AREA: 2.8m^2

BOILER PRESSURE: 12kg/cm^2

SUPERHEATED

ITALY   0–6–0T RACK AND ADHESION   1435mm

Four-cylinder 0–6–0 rack and adhesion Side Tank locomotive No 980.006 a sister engine of No 980.002 which is preserved   [J. D. Blyth]

No 980.002 was originally No 9802 and later 98002. It was built for FS in 1908 by SLM (works number 1898), one of 12 rack and adhesion 0–6–0T, to work on the steeply graded line between Paola and Cosenza. It is a four-cylinder compound with all four cylinders and their slide valves outside the frames. The low pressure cylinders drive the rack pinions through reduction gearing and these cylinders are placed above the high pressure cylinders driving the adhesion wheels on each side. The rack system is Riggenbach. When the locomotive was in use on the more level sections of the line, the high pressure cylinders only were used, the locomotive then working as a two-cylinder simple. On the rack sections it was used as a four-cylinder compound. Walschaerts valve gear is provided for both high and low pressure cylinders, the die blocks of the expansion links being connected for compound working.

This locomotive is at present stored at Rome, Smistamento Depot.
Dimensions: CYLINDERS: HIGH PRESSURE: 430 × 500mm
                                    LOW PRESSURE: 430 × 500mm
                COUPLED WHEELS: 1040mm
                GRATE AREA: 1.8m²
                BOILER PRESSURE: 14kg/cm²

39

Narrow Gauge Locomotive Preservation in Italy

Narrow gauge railways in Italy were built, for the most part, in the southern part of the country, and in the islands of Sicily and Sardinia. They were, and are, operated both by the State Railways, FS, and by private railway companies who, in their prime, owned about 2,750km of narrow gauge track.

Most narrow gauge railways were constructed to a gauge of 950mm which the Government laid down as the standard for such lines. In Sicily, it was necessary to incorporate a number of rack sections which were worked by four-cylinder compound rack and adhesion 0–6–0 Side Tanks and the Strub rack system was used.

There were a few 760mm-gauge lines owned both privately and by the State. One of the best known of these was the Val Gardena line in the Dolomites.

Only four narrow gauge locomotives are known to be preserved or intended for preservation. Two ran on the 760mm gauge and two on the 950mm gauge.

None of them is of outstanding technical interest.

No R410.004 of the Plan Val Gardena   [P. M. Kalla-Bishop Collection

No R 410.004 is an outside cylinder 0–8–0 Well Tank locomotive with outside frames which was built in 1916 by Krauss (works number 7174) as No 4154 Class IVc for the *KUK Heeresbahn* (Austro-Hungarian Military Railways).

Seven of these locomotives worked on the 31km Val Gardena line between Chiusa and Plan in the Dolomites. This line was built as a military railway during World War I by Russian prisoners-of-war and it had the distinction of being the highest line operated by FS with a summit at 1595m above sea level.

No R 410.004 is at Rome, Smistamento Depot in store pending preservation and display.

Dimensions: CYLINDERS: 320 × 350mm
              COUPLED WHEELS: 800mm
              GRATE AREA: 1.0m²
              BOILER PRESSURE: 12kg/cm²

No P 7 is an 0–8–2T which was built in 1922 by Officine Meccaniche Reggio Emilia (works number 117) for the FS line which ran southwards from Trieste Aquilinia up to Parenzo. This line was closed in 1935 and the locomotives, with the exception of No P 7, were converted to 950mm gauge and sent to work in Sicily. No P 7 was intended for war service on the 760mm lines in Jugoslavia but was never sent there and has been in store until it has now been put on exhibition in the Museum of Science and Technology in Milan.

No P 7 and her sisters were identical with the Austrian kkStB Class P of 1911.

Dimensions: CYLINDERS: 330 × 400mm
COUPLED WHEELS: 880mm
GRATE AREA: 1.3m^2
BOILER PRESSURE: 13kg/cm^2
SUPERHEATED

No R301.027 which is identical with the preserved locomotive   [P. R-W

No R301.2 was originally FS No 302 and is a 2–6–0T which was built in 1912 by Costruzioni Meccaniche Saronno (works number 461) for the Sicilian narrow-gauge lines. It has outside cylinders with slide valves and is not superheated. Thirty-three of the class were built for service in Eritrea as well as in Sicily. They could achieve a maximum speed of 50km/h.

No R301.2 is now exhibited in the Museum of Science and Technology, Milan.

Dimensions: CYLINDERS: 380 × 450mm
            COUPLED WHEELS: 950mm
            GRATE AREA: 1.2m^2
            BOILER PRESSURE: 12kg/cm^2

No R302.027 is the same as the preserved locomotive. The fuel oil tank is seen in front of the dome
[P. R-W

No R302.23 was built in 1927 by Officine Meccaniche e Navali, Napoli (works number 104) for the narrow-gauge lines in Sicily. Forty-two of these 2–6–0T locomotives were built and they were a modernised, and more powerful superheated version of Group R301. Many locomotives of both groups carried large fuel oil tanks on top of the boiler behind the chimney and could be fired either by coal or by oil and coal.

No R302.23 is at present in store at Rome, Smistamento Depot.

Dimensions: CYLINDERS: 410 × 450mm
COUPLED WHEELS: 950mm
GRATE AREA: 1.2m^2
BOILER PRESSURE: 12kg/cm^2
SUPERHEATED

Netherlands Railway Company

The *NV Nederlandsche Spoorwegen* (NS) came into existence on January 1,
1938, by taking over complete control and ownership of all railways in
Holland. Previously, the railways had been owned by two major
companies which had, themselves, been state-controlled since 1920 and
were collectively known as *Nederlandsche Spoorwegen* (NS). The Companies
concerned were the *Hollandsche Ijzeren Spoorweg Maatschappij*—Holland
Iron Railway Company, known as the Holland Railway Company
(HSM), and the *Maatschappij tot Exploitate van Staatsspoorwegen*—
Company for the Running of State Railways, known as the State
Railways (SS). These two Companies had, over the years, absorbed most
other smaller railways of which the most important were the
Netherlands Rhenish Railway in 1890 (the assets of this company were
divided between the two big companies), the Netherlands Central
Railway (NCS) and the North Brabant Railway (NBDS) both of which
were taken over by the State Railways in 1919.

Locomotive Preservation in
the Netherlands

The principal collection of preserved steam locomotives is in the
Netherlands Railway Museum which is housed in the old Maliebaan-
station, Joan van Oldenbarneveltlaan 6, Utrecht. The museum also
contains a very fine collection of models, railway relics and thematic
postage stamps.

A smaller Light Railway Museum is at Enschede where there are five
1435mm-gauge steam tank locomotives, all of which are to be preserved
in working order but of which three are industrial engines.

The Netherlands Tramway Society known as *Tramweg-Stichting* own
several Steam Tram locomotives of both standard and 1067mm-gauge
and they can operate over the old NS single line branch between Hoorn
and Medemblik on the Zuyder Zee.

One locomotive is also preserved in the village of Bergen.

Netherlands Steam Locomotives

Most steam locomotives were characterised by their elegance and beauty of design. The livery of the NS was apple-green fully lined-out, with copper chimney tops and polished brass dome and safety valve covers for passenger engines.

The Classification of NS locomotives was easy to follow:

P represented passenger locomotives

G   ,,   goods (freight) ,,

R   ,,   shunting   ,,

L   ,,   branch line   ,,

T   ,,   tank   ,,

O indicated that the engine was superheated.

Thus, for example, Class GTO/3 was a superheated goods tank locomotive of Series 3.

Full-scale replica of DE AREND   [Railway Museum, Utrecht

No 2 *DE AREND* (The Eagle) was one of the first two locomotives in Holland. It was an inside-cylinder 2-2-2 built in 1839 by Longridge of Bedlington, England, works number 119. (The Italian locomotive *BAYARD* (qv) was works number 120.) Engine No 1 *SNELHEID* (Speed) was actually the first locomotive in Holland and worked the first train between Amsterdam and Haarlem. *DE AREND* was scrapped in 1857 but a working full-size replica was built in 1938 in the Central Workshops of the NS at Zwolle for the Railway Centenary Celebrations of 1939. This replica is now in the Utrecht Railway Museum.

The first railway in Holland was opened between Amsterdam and Haarlem in 1839, this being the first part of the *Hollandsche Ijzeren Spoorweg Maatschappij* (the Holland Iron Railway Company). It was laid to a gauge of 2000mm and was not altered to 1435mm-gauge until 1866.

Four similar, but not identical, 2-2-2 locomotives were delivered to the railway in 1839 by Longridge. In particular, No 2 *DE AREND* and No 4 *LEEUW* (Lion) had smaller driving wheels and larger cylinders than had the other two and they were 1.5 tonnes heavier. These two engines had gab valve gear.

Dimensions: CYLINDERS: 356 × 450mm
             DRIVING WHEELS: 1810mm
             GRATE AREA: 1.1m^2
             BOILER PRESSURE: 4kg/cm^2

47

No 13 preserved in the Railway Museum   [Railway Museum, Utrecht

No 13 is an inside-cylinder 2–4–0 with Allan link motion operating slide valves between the cylinders. It was built in 1864 by Beyer, Peacock (works number 533) for the State Railways (SS) and is at present preserved in its original condition in the Railway Museum at Utrecht.

Thirty-three of these locomotives were delivered to the railway in 1865 and others at a later date. They were all later provided with cabs and air brakes.

Two of the engines, Nos 12 and 14, had four-wheeled tenders, the others had low-sided six-wheel tenders which were ultimately enlarged with high sides and increased tank and bunker capacity. The tender now behind No 13 was originally behind the ill-fated No 8 which suffered a boiler explosion at Harlingen in 1868. The locomotive was repaired at Manchester but was withdrawn in 1884.

Dimensions: CYLINDERS: 406 × 508mm
              COUPLED WHEELS: 1700mm
              GRATE AREA: 1.4m^2
              BOILER PRESSURE: 8.3kg/cm^2

No 89 NESTOR [Railway Musuem, Utrecht

No 89 *NESTOR* is an outside-cylinder 2–4–0 built in 1880 by Borsig (works number 3730) for the Holland Railway Company (HSM) and now preserved in the Railway Museum at Utrecht.

Twenty-nine of these locomotives were built by Borsig between 1878 and 1883 and, in accordance with HSM practice, all were named, the last nine after famous Dutchmen. They had Belpaire fireboxes, Rams-bottom safety valves and large wooden-sided cabs, the reason for the latter being to reduce the high noise level inherent in cabs with sides of iron plates. The names were removed from all the HSM locomotives when the Company was amalgamated in 1921 with the other three large railway companies.

Borsig supplied many outside-cylinder 2–4–0s to HSM and they provide an interesting contrast with the many inside-cylinder 2–4–0s supplied contemporaneously by Beyer, Peacock to the State Railway Company (SS).

Dimensions: CYLINDERS: 406 × 558mm
                COUPLED WHEELS: 1860mm
                GRATE AREA: 1.6m²
                BOILER PRESSURE: 10.3kg/cm²

2–4–0 No 326

No 326 is an inside-cylinder 2–4–0 built in 1881 by Beyer, Peacock (works number 2101) for the State Railways (SS). It is preserved in the Utrecht Railway Museum.

The association between Messrs. Beyer, Peacock and the State Railways was very close and of long duration. It resulted in the design and production of one of the most successful locomotive classes ever to run in the Netherlands. Mr. J. W. Stous Sloot was Chief Mechanical Engineer of the SS and, in collaboration with Beyer, Peacock, the 2–4–0 engines Nos 301–317 appeared in 1880. Over the next 15 years, a total of 176 of these locomotives was built, three of which went to the North Brabant Railway. They became Class P/3 of the NS, and their old numbers, 301–475, were altered to 1301–1475. In 1892, Beyer, Peacock built one engine, No 701 as a two-cylinder compound with inside Walschaerts valve gear. The economies were insignificant and no more were built.

The 301 Class were the first engines on the SS to have Belpaire fire-boxes. They had inside Stephenson link motion with slide valves between the cylinders. The leading axle was fitted with Cartazzi axle-boxes allowing 12.5mm side movement in each direction. Compared with the large wood-sided cabs of the HSM 2–4–0s (qv) the SS cabs were, to say the least, rather austere.

During 1883, comparative trials of coal consumption and maintenance costs were made between these 2–4–0 express engines and 0–6–0 freight engines of Series 161–205 hauling 570-tonne coal trains at 30km/h on a level track. The 2–4–0s proved to be slightly the more economical and, as a result, they were used successfully for many years, as true mixed traffic engines, handling express and freight trains with equal facility.

Dimensions: CYLINDERS: 457 × 660mm   GRATE AREA: 2.2m^2
COUPLED WHEELS: 2134mm   BOILER PRESSURE: 10.3kg/cm^2

4–4–0 No 107   [Railway Museum, Utrecht

No 107 is an inside-cylinder 4–4–0 which was built in 1881 by Sharp Stewart (works number 3563) for the Netherlands Rhenish Railway. It is restored to its original condition and is painted in the Rhenish Railway colours of chocolate brown with red frames and wheels. No 107 is now in the Railway Museum at Utrecht.

The Netherlands Rhenish Railway (NRS) which also owned most of the shares of the Netherlands Central Railway, was taken over by the two major companies, the Holland Railway Company (HSM) and the State Railways Company (SS), in October 1890. The last locomotives to be built for the NRS were nine 4–4–0s Nos 101–109 and of which No 107 is a survivor. Of these engines Nos 101–103 and 108–109 went to the SS and Nos 104–107 to the HSM. In 1891, however, the HSM took over the five engines from the SS and the class became HSM Nos 350–358 and, later, NS Nos 1601–1609 Class P/3.

When the NRS received these nine engines in 1889, they were the first bogie engines in Holland and the first British-built bogie engines in Continental Europe. They had slide valves driven by Stephenson link motion. They were good engines of a straightforward design and between 1891 and 1903 a further 50 were built for HSM. Some of these were later superheated and became NS Class PO/1.

Dimensions: CYLINDERS: 457 × 660mm
                COUPLED WHEELS: 2016mm
                GRATE AREA: 2.2m^2
                BOILER PRESSURE: 10.3kg/cm^2

4–4–0 No 2104 in the Railway Museum   [Railway Museum, Utrecht

No 2104 is an inside-cylinder superheated 4–4–0 built in 1914 as No 504 of the Holland Railway Company (HSM) by Schwartzkopff (works number 5304). It is preserved in the Railway Museum, Utrecht and carries its NS number. It was NS Class PO/2.

The 35 large 4–4–0s were designed by W. Hupkes, Chief Mechanical Engineer of HSM and 15 were built by Schwartzkopff, the remainder by Werkspoor. Delivery was interrupted by World War I and the class was not completed until 1920.

The engines were required to haul trains of 400 tonnes at an average speed of 90km/h for a distance of 200km without having to take water, and this they were well able to do. They had some innovations for Holland. Hochwald piston valves (later replaced by normal narrow-ring piston valves) were driven by inside Walschaerts valve gear and the regulators were of the Zara type. Although the axle load was 17 tonnes, the factor of adhesion was low, being only 4.8. As a result, on a wet rail with a heavy load, it was difficult to prevent their slipping.

Dimensions: CYLINDERS: 530 × 660mm
            COUPLED WHEELS: 2100mm
            GRATE AREA: 2.4m^2
            BOILER PRESSURE: 12.4kg/cm^2
            SUPERHEATED

Four-cylinder 4–6–0 No 3737   [Railway Museum, Utrecht

No 3737 is a four-cylinder superheated 4–6–0 built in 1911 by Werkspoor (works number 272)* as No 731 for the State Railways (SS). This was the last steam locomotive to work on a scheduled train in Holland and it is now preserved in the Railway Museum at Utrecht.

These locomotives were among the most beautiful of any in Europe and they were powerful, quiet and efficient. They were designed at the Gorton Foundry, Manchester by Beyer, Peacock, the requirement being for a locomotive for heavy main-line passenger duties at speeds not exceeding 90km/h and with a maximum axle-load of 16 tonnes. This could be accepted as the balanced four-cylinder arrangement eradicates hammer-blow. The four cylinders were in line and all drove the leading coupled axle. Two sets of Walschaerts valve gear were inside the frames and drove the inside-cylinder piston valves. The outside valves were driven from the tail rods of the inside valves through horizontal rocking levers. The tractive effort at 65 per cent mean effective pressure was 8900kg.

One hundred and twenty of these engines were built, 36 by Beyer, Peacock between 1910 and 1914, 54 by Werkspoor between 1911 and 1921, 25 by Hanomag and Henschel in 1920–21 and five by Schwartzkopff in 1928. These last five engines had eight-wheeled tenders.

Dimensions: CYLINDERS (4): 400 × 660mm
            COUPLED WHEELS: 1850mm
            GRATE AREA: 2.8m^2
            BOILER PRESSURE: 12kg/cm^2
            SUPERHEATED

* *As preserved, it carries, in error, the works plate of Werkspoor No 281 of 1911.*

2–10–0 No 73755 LONGMOOR   [Railway Museum, Utrecht

No 73755 *LONGMOOR* is a superheated 2–10–0 locomotive built in 1945 by North British (works number 25601) for the British War Department. It is one of 150 2–10–0s built to the design of R. A. Riddles as "Austerity" locomotives during World War II. It is now preserved at the Railway Museum, Utrecht.

The name plate of the locomotive commemorates the Longmoor Military Railway in Hampshire, England and also states that this was the 1,000th locomotive built in Britain for War needs.

In 1945–46, the Netherlands Railways received, on loan, 103 of these locomotives which they numbered 5001–5103, *LONGMOOR* being NS No 5085. It came to Holland from Belgium, having worked, for a short time, on the SNCB from Tournai Depot.

Dimensions: CYLINDERS: 483 × 711mm
        COUPLED WHEELS: 1435mm
        GRATE AREA: 3.7m^2
        BOILER PRESSURE: 15.8kg/cm^2
        SUPERHEATED

0–4–0T No 8107 in the Enschede Museum [Enschede Museum

NS No 8107 is an 0–4–0 Side Tank locomotive with outside cylinders and Walschaerts valvegear which was built in 1901 by Backer and Rueb, Breda (works number 170) as No 657 of the State Railways (SS). It is now preserved in working order by the *Stichting Museum Buurt Spoorweg* at Enschede.

The coal bunker was over the right-hand side tank and some of the engines had shorter tanks than those of No 8107.

On the NS, these locomotives carried a double classification—R/2, L/3 indicating that they could be used for shunting or for branch line duties. They originally had copper-topped, bell-mouth chimneys.

Dimensions: CYLINDERS: 370 × 480mm

COUPLED WHEELS: 1100mm

GRATE AREA: 1.2m^2

BOILER PRESSURE: 11.7kg/cm^2

0–6–0WT No 7742 on display at Bergen   [P. R-W Collection

NS No 7742 is an 0–6–0 Well Tank locomotive built as No 1046 of the Holland Railway Company in 1914 by Schwartzkopff (works number 5249).

It is preserved and is on display in the centre of the village of Bergen.

This is one of 44 locomotives of NS Class L/3 built between 1905 and 1914 by Werkspoor, Henschel and Schwartzkopff for suburban passenger services. Slide valves above the cylinders were operated by outside Allan link motion. The engines had steam sanding gear, the Henry direct acting brake and also the Westinghouse automatic brake.

The last nine engines, of which No 7742 is one, were also fitted with the vacuum brake, modified buffers, couplings and steam heat connections to enable them to work with (steam) tramways rolling stock.

Dimensions: CYLINDERS: 330 × 550mm

         COUPLED WHEELS: 1230mm

         GRATE AREA: 1.3m^2

         BOILER PRESSURE: 12.4kg/cm^2

Four-cylinder 4–8–4 back tank No 6317 in the Railway Museum   [Railway Museum, Utrecht

No 6317 Class GTO/3 is a four-cylinder 4–8–4 Back Tank locomotive which was built for the Netherlands Railways in 1931 by Schwartzkopff (works number 10056)*. It is now preserved in the Railway Museum at Utrecht.

Twenty-two of these locomotives were built, ten by Henschel in 1930 and 12 by Schwartzkopff in 1931. With a weight in working order of 126.4 tonnes and a tractive effort (70 per cent MEP) 14,700kg these were, in 1930, the heaviest and most powerful non-articulated tank engines in Europe.

The four cylinders, in line, all drove the leading coupled axle; they had piston valves above them, the inside valves being driven direct by two sets of Walschaerts gear inside the frames and the outside valves were driven through horizontal rocking shafts by the tail rods of the inside valves. Cylinders, motion, cranked axle, boiler and some other details were all interchangeable with those of the large four-cylinder 4–6–0 express locomotives of the 3900 Series and, as in those locomotives, the frames were of the bar type. Water was carried in a back tank below the coal bunker over the trailing bogie.

These locomotives were built for working coal and mineral trains from the South Limburg area to Utrecht and other points north. They could,

* *As preserved, it carries in error the works plate of Schwartzkopff No 10059 of 1931.*

on occasion, work heavy passenger trains, their coupled wheels of 1550mm allowing speeds of up to 90km/h.

Dimensions: CYLINDERS (4): 420 × 660mm
COUPLED WHEELS: 1550mm
GRATE AREA: 3.2m²
BOILER PRESSURE: 14kg/cm²
SUPERHEATED

NETHERLANDS   0–4–0 Tram   1435mm

RSTM No 2 in the Railway Museum   [Railway Museum, Utrecht

Rhenish Steam Tram Company (RSTM) No 2 is an inside-cylinder 0–4–0 Tram engine built in 1881 by Merryweather (works number 110). It is preserved in the Railway Museum at Utrecht.

The Netherland Rhenish Railway main line ran in a south-easterly direction across Holland from Amsterdam to Utrecht and on to Emmerich in Germany. In 1879 and 1882, the company opened two standard gauge steam tramways: the first between The Hague and Scheveningen (4.7km) and the second between Ede and Wageningen (7.1km). To work these tramways, 17 0–4–0 Tram engines, of two classes, were built by Merryweather of London, the differences between Class 18 and Class 19 being in the boiler pressures and heating surfaces. No 2 (preserved) is of Class 19.

The design of all steam tram engines in Holland was influenced by an Act of the City of Hague which decreed, among other things, that the cylinders should be between the frames and that a skirting of iron sheets should protect the coupled wheels, the object being to prevent the frightening of horses. No 2 and her sisters have two inside cylinders with slide valves operated by Stephenson link motion.

The water is carried mainly in a large tank in the roof of the locomotive and arrangements are made so that, by the operation of a slide valve in the bottom of the blast pipe, the exhaust steam may be deflected into the water tank and condensed. Similar arrangements are made to deflect steam from the safety valves into the smokebox. This was again decreed and was again to avoid frightening horses. The boiler is fed by one injector and an eccentric-driven feed pump.

The engines originally had steam brakes and foot brakes but later were fitted with vacuum brakes and more powerful foot brakes.

Dimensions: CYLINDERS: 178 × 279.5mm
COUPLED WHEELS: 739mm
GRATE AREA: 0.4m^2
BOILER PRESSURE: 10.3kg/cm^2

Gooische Steam Tram No 18 with 0–4–0WT No 30 (ex Gas works, Rotterdam) hauling special train on the tracks of the Westlandsche Stoomtram Mij [F. van der Gragt

Gooische Steam Tramway Company No 18 is an inside-cylinder 0–4–0 Steam Tram locomotive built in 1921 by Henschel (works number 18776). It follows normal Dutch steam tram design and is now named *LEEGHWATER*; it is owned by the *Tramweg-Stichting* for use on their Hoorn-Medemblik line.

Dimensions: NOT KNOWN

No 22 is an inside-cylinder 0–4–0 Steam Tram locomotive which was built in 1904 for the Tramway Company of The Hague (*Haagsche Tramweg Maatschappij*) as their No 8 by Backer and Rueb (works number 227). It was later sold to the Tramway Company of North and South Holland (*Nord-Zuid-Hollandsche Tramweg Maatschappij*) as their No 12. This company, in turn, sold the little engine to the Company for the Exploitation of Brown Coalfields "Carisborg" Ltd. who numbered it 22. It finally returned to its builders and is now preserved in a garden at the works of *NV Machinefabriek* "Breda" (formerly Backer and Rueb).

This little tram engine was superheated and was fitted with condensing arrangements in the tanks on the roof. It had vacuum brakes.

Dimensions: CYLINDERS: 225 × 350mm
COUPLED WHEELS: 800mm
GRATE AREA: 0.68m²
BOILER PRESSURE: 14.47kg/cm²
SUPERHEATED

Narrow Gauge Locomotive Preservation in the Netherlands

NETHERLANDS   0–6–0 Tram   1067mm

RTM 0–6–0WT No 57 in the Railway Museum   [Railway Museum, Utrecht

Four Rotterdam Tramway Company (RTM) inside-cylinder 0–6–0 Well Tank locomotives are preserved. Three of them are now owned by The Tramway Society (*Tramweg-Stichting*) and are stored at Hellevoetsluis. These are No 50 (Henschel 11722 of 1913), No 54 (Orenstein 8065 of 1915) and No 56 (Orenstein 9193 of 1920). No 57 (Orenstein 9194 of 1920) is restored and is in the Railway Museum, Utrecht.

These locomotives have two well tanks, one on each side below the running plates. The tanks are outside the coupled wheels and act as wheel guards in place of the more usual sheet-iron plates. Arrangements are made by which the exhaust steam can be deflected into the tanks and condensed.

Dimensions: CYLINDERS: 330 × 400mm
COUPLED WHEELS: 885mm
GRATE AREA: 0.8m²
BOILER PRESSURE: 14kg/cm²

ZE Steam Tram No 607 VRIJLAND in the Railway Museum   [Railway Museum, Utrecht

Zutphen-Emmerich Tramway Company (ZE) No 607 *VRIJLAND* is an inside-cylinder 0–4–0 steam tram locomotive which was built in 1904 by Henschel (works number 6848). It is preserved in the Railway Museum at Utrecht.

Holland had many steam-operated tramways of several different gauges and there was a great variety of them in the southern part of the country. The Zutphen-Emmerich, however, qualified as an international line for, although most of the tramway was in Holland, the southern terminus of the line, Emmerich, is in Germany.

No 607 conforms to the requirements of a tramway locomotive in Holland in that it has inside cylinders and protective casings around the wheels, and that the exhaust steam can be turned into the side tanks.

Dimensions: CYLINDERS: 260 × 320mm
COUPLED WHEELS: 750mm
GRATE AREA: 0.6m²
BOILER PRESSURE: 14kg/cm²

Norwegian State Railways
Norges Statsbanen (NSB)

The first railway in Norway was a 1435mm-gauge line which was opened
on September 1, 1854, between Christiana (after 1925 known as Oslo)
and Eidsvoll, a distance of 68km. It was built by a private company
with mostly British capital though the State owned some of the shares.
Robert Stephenson was the engineer. As a result of a law of 1857, the
State was empowered to finance new railway construction and, in view
of the difficult terrain, a gauge of 1067mm was chosen for many of the
new lines. Private railways, however, also continued to be built and the
Oslo-Eidsvoll line, now known as the *Norske Hoved Jernbane* (Norwegian
Trunk Line) remained independent until taken over by NSB in 1926.
For many years, however, a journey from Christiana to Trondheim
involved a change of trains at Hamar, from the 1435mm to the 1067mm
gauge.

By 1883 Norway had 1552km of railway of which 960km were narrow
gauge, but for the next 15 years there was little new construction. From
the turn of the century, there was increasing conversion of the 1067mm
lines to 1435mm gauge and by the Centenary year, 1954, the route
kilometres of all Norwegian railways was 3968 of which 807km was
narrow gauge. Only 163km were privately owned and 17km of this
latter total was of 1435mm gauge.

Most of the lines south of Oslo, the Narvik iron-ore line, the
Bergen line and the Hamar-Dombas-Trondheim line are now electrified
with single-phase ac 15kV, $16\frac{2}{3}$ c/s. Other trunk routes and the
Dombas-Andalsnes line are diesel operated.

Steam Locomotive Preservation
in Norway

The principal collection of railway relics is at Hamar in a museum owned
by NSB and situated on a site of generous proportions beside Lake Mjøsa
on the north side of the town. The museum was started more than 75
years ago but it has been re-housed twice, before being finally re-settled
in its present location. There is room for many more exhibits and it is
hoped that one or two more steam locomotives of essentially Norwegian
design, may be restored in future though none is at present scheduled.

An attractive feature of the Railway Museum at Hamar is the
provision of a 750-mm gauge track, some 350m in length on which a
locomotive is occasionally steamed.

No 17 CAROLINE   [P. R-W

No 16 and No 17 *CAROLINE* are outside-cylinder 2–4–0 locomotives with inside Stephenson link motion operating slide valves. They were built in 1861 for the *Norsk Hoved Jernbane* (Norwegian Trunk Railway) by Robert Stephenson (works numbers 1406 and 1407 respectively). Both engines are now preserved in the Railway Museum at Hamar.

No 17 was sold by the *Hoved Jernbane* in 1919 to *Klevfoss Cellulosfabrik* and was re-purchased by NSB in 1953 to participate in the 1954 Railway Centenary celebrations. On that occasion it was in steam and it also worked at other places in Norway during that year, hauling a train of contemporary coaches.

Robert Stephenson supplied, in 1851, the first locomotives to work in Norway. These were also outside-cylinder 2–4–0s for the *Hoved Jernbane* and they had larger cylinders but lower boiler pressure than the 1861 engines.

Dimensions of Nos 16 and 17: CYLINDERS: 305 × 508mm
                     COUPLED WHEELS: 1435mm
                     GRATE AREA: 0.75m²
                     BOILER PRESSURE: 9.8kg/cm²

No 207 Class 21e is an outside-cylinder 2–6–0 locomotive which was built in 1909 by Hamar (works number 36). It is to go to the Railway Museum at Hamar.

No 224 Class 21b identical with No 377   [P. R-W

No 377 Class 21b is an outside-cylinder 2–6–0 locomotive which was built in 1919 by Nydquist (works number 1164). This locomotive hauled the coach in which the late King of Norway travelled to the north, and safety, during the German invasion of his country in 1940. It has been purchased for the Bressingham Steam Museum at Diss, Norfolk and it arrived at its destination in 1970. It now carries the name *HAAKON VII.*

The NSB used its 2–6–0 locomotives mainly for operating over the lightly laid track of its branch lines and they were simple and economical machines with a maximum axle-load of about 10 tonnes. (This varied a little between sub-classes.)

There were 45 engines of Class 21 of which the earliest were built in 1905 as two-cylinder compounds (Class 21a). Later engines of Classes 21b, 21c, 21d and 21e were all two-cylinder simples with Walschaerts valve gear and round-topped boilers and the last were built from 1919 onwards. Some were equipped to burn wood and had spark arresting chimneys.

The main differences between the sub-classes were in the boiler heating surfaces and, in consequence, the weights varied slightly. They were very similar in dimensions to the 2–6–0 engines of Standard Class 2 on British Railways.

Dimensions: CYLINDERS: 432 × 610mm
COUPLED WHEELS: 1445mm
GRATE AREA: 1.78m^2
BOILER PRESSURE: 12kg/cm^2
SUPERHEATED

No 134 Class 18c is the same type and class as No 255　　　　　[NSB

No 255 Class 18c is an outside cylinder 4–6–0 built in 1913 by Hamar (works number 84). It is at present in store but is scheduled for preservation.

Between 1900 and 1916, 35 light-weight mixed traffic 4–6–0s were built for NSB, the first eight by Chemnitz and the rest by Hamar. They were able to work over nearly the whole system, having a maximum axle-load only slightly in excess of 12 tonnes. The safety valves were on the dome and the sand dome was behind and separate from the steam dome.

Nineteen of the engines were built as von Borries two-cylinder compounds with balanced slide valves using saturated steam. The rest were built as simples with piston valves and, later, superheaters. The compounds were classified 18a and 18b, there being minor differences in heating surfaces and weights between the sub-classes. The simples were 18c. There were only two compounds in the Chemnitz batch, another appeared in 1903 and then, from 1907 to 1911 all the 16 engines built were compounds. After that, the rest were built as simples. Nine compounds of both sub-classes were converted to simples of Class 18c and, in 1927, two were rebuilt completely to Class 27 (qv).

Dimensions (Class 18c): CYLINDERS: 480 × 650mm
　　　　　　　　　　COUPLED WHEELS: 1445mm
　　　　　　　　　　GRATE AREA: 1.9m²
　　　　　　　　　　BOILER PRESSURE: 13kg/cm²
　　　　　　　　　　SUPERHEATED

A locomotive of Class 27a, No 296 [NSB

No 234 Class 27a is a 4–6–0 passenger locomotive with outside cylinders which is to be preserved.

No 234 is one of two locomotives, Nos 234 and 235, which were built in 1911 by Hamar (works numbers 66 and 67 respectively) as two-cylinder von Borries compounds of Class 18b. They were rebuilt to Class 27 in 1927 with larger coupled wheels and with two simple cylinders with piston valves retaining their Walschaerts valve gear. They were then superheated.

The original 15 locomotives of Class 27 were built between 1910 and 1921. They were the lightweight passenger engine development of Class 18c but, though more modern, were less powerful. The steam dome, with the safety valves on top, was in the same casing as the sand dome.

Dimensions: CYLINDERS: 450 × 600mm
        COUPLED WHEELS: 1600mm
        GRATE AREA: 1.5m²
        BOILER PRESSURE: 12kg/cm²
        SUPERHEATED

C

A locomotive of Class 30a on a south-bound express leaving Otta   [P. R-W

No 271 Class 30a is a four-cylinder simple superheated 4–6–0 locomotive built in 1914 by Thunes (works number 82). It is to be preserved and is at present stored.

Between 1913 and 1919, 18 of these engines were built by Thunes for dealing with fast passenger services on the, then, new line to Trondheim on which speeds of up to 90km/h were allowed on some sections.

The four cylinders are in line, all driving the leading coupled axle. One piston valve is provided for the two cylinders on each side, the cranks being at 180 deg to each other. It is thus possible for the single piston valve to admit steam to the back of one cylinder and to the front of the other by means of crossed ports. Two sets of Walschaerts valve gear drive the two piston valves.

Between 1919 and 1939 a further 34 engines of Class 30b were built but these were four-cylinder compounds and had a higher boiler pressure (16kg/cm²). The method of steam distribution was the same as for the simple engines.

Dimensions (of Class 30a): CYLINDERS (4): 390 × 600mm
                               COUPLED WHEELS: 1600mm
                               GRATE AREA: 2.4m²
                               BOILER PRESSURE: 12kg/cm²
                               SUPERHEATED

No 418 of Class 31b   [P. R-W

No 452 Class 31b is a four-cylinder compound superheated 4–8–0 which was built in 1926 by Hamar (works number 334). It is at present stored and awaiting preservation.

Twenty-seven of these heavy, 4–8–0 locomotives were built between 1921 and 1926 for passenger services on the Oslo-Bergen line. They were preceded by four similar engines (two built in 1915 and two in 1921) but which were four-cylinder simples of Class 30a. In both the simples and the compounds a single piston valve was provided for each pair of cylinders on each side. The ports were crossed, and the cranks of each pair were at 180 deg to each other and at 90 deg to those of the other side. The valves were driven by Walschaerts valve gear. All four cylinders drove the second coupled axle, the low pressure cylinders being outside and the high pressure inside, the plate frames. A starting valve allowed high pressure steam to enter the low pressure cylinders.

The cabs of all these engines were totally enclosed and were provided with steel bars in front of the spectacles to protect the glasses from hard snow which was thrown up when the engines ran into drifts.

The 4–8–0 type was introduced into Norway in 1910 when the first of Class 26 came from SLM. Over the years both simples and compounds were built, all with a maximum axle-load of only 11.6 tonnes. Engines of Class 31b, with a 14-tonne axle-load were the largest and heaviest of the NSB 4–8–0s.

Dimensions: CYLINDERS: HIGH PRESSURE: 420 × 600mm
                             LOW PRESSURE: 630 × 600mm
        COUPLED WHEELS: 1350mm
        GRATE AREA: 3.0m^2
        BOILER PRESSURE: 16kg/cm^2
        SUPERHEATED

No 472 Class 49c was the same as the preserved locomotive [P. R-W

No 470 *DOVREGUBBEN* Class 49c is a four-cylinder compound 2-8-4 built in 1940 by Krupp (works number 2152). It now carries the number and works plates of No 471 (Krupp works number 2153 of 1940). It is preserved and is on display in the Railway Museum at Hamar.

In 1935-36 three large four-cylinder compound 2-8-4 locomotives were built by Thunes Mekaniske Vaerksted for service between Dombas and Trondheim, the most difficult and heavily graded part of the route from Oslo to the north. As the route for which these engines were designed passes over the Dovre Mountain, the first of the Class was named *DOVREGUBBEN* (Dovre Giant).

The two high pressure cylinders were inside the frames, and the low pressure cylinders outside. Two sets of outside Heusinger valve gear were provided, each set driving one low pressure and one high pressure piston valve, the latter through a rocking shaft. These three engines had double blast pipes and chimneys. In order to keep the maximum axle-load down to 15.6 tonnes, dimensions of materials had to be kept to a minimum and plate frames were used. The first two locomotives, Nos 463 and 464 were Class 49a, the third, No 465, was provided with a booster on the trailing truck and was Class 49b. The booster was later removed.

At the time of the German Occupation in 1940, four more of these locomotives were on order, two from Krupp and two from Thunes. These were delivered in 1940 (Nos 470 and 471) and 1941 (Nos 472 and 473)

respectively and were Class 49c. They had single blast-pipes and chimneys and the diameter of both high pressure and low pressure cylinders was less than that of the previous locomotives.

No 470, the preserved locomotive, has had the name plates of No 463 transferred to it. Many regret that it has not been possible to preserve one of the original three 2–8–4s.

Dimensions: CYLINDERS: HIGH PRESSURE: 440 × 650mm
LOW PRESSURE: 650 × 700mm
COUPLED WHEELS: 1530mm
GRATE AREA: 5.0m^2
BOILER PRESSURE: 17kg/cm^2
SUPERHEATED

No 62 Class 7a was identical with No 25 and with No 11   [P. R-W

No 25 *ULKE* Class 7a is an 0–4–0 Square Saddle Tank locomotive built in 1875 for the NSB by Manning Wardle (works number 576). It is preserved in the Railway Museum at Hamar.

No 11 of the same class will also be preserved in the new station at Oslo.

According to some authorities, these engines were built originally for the 1067mm gauge and later converted to 1435mm but confirmation is lacking.

These engines had domeless boilers and the valve gear was inside Stephenson link motion.

Dimensions: CYLINDERS: 254 × 406mm
COUPLED WHEELS: 990mm
GRATE AREA: 1.10m^2
BOILER PRESSURE: 9kg/cm^2

No 424 Class 25d [P. R-W

No 424 Class 25d is a superheated o–6–o Well Tank locomotive with piston valves which was built in 1923 by Hamar (works number 304). It is to be preserved in working order by the Norwegian Railway Club, reputably for the working of excursion trains on its standard gauge line.

No 227 Class 25a is an o–6–o Well Tank locomotive which was built in 1910 by Hamar (works number 60). It is not superheated and has balanced slide valves. It will be preserved in the Hamar Railway Museum.

c–6–o Well Tanks were the standard shunting engines of the NSB, and 28 of Class 25 were built for NSB between 1909 and 1923. The sub-classes varied in detail, but all of the engines were very similar to five of Class 25e which came to NSB from the Swiss Federal Railways (ex Jura-Simplon) in 1947 and were built by SLM in 1901.

The four engines of Class 25d, however, were the only ones which were superheated.

Dimensions: CYLINDERS: 360 × 500mm
COUPLED WHEELS: 1060mm
GRATE AREA: 1.17m²
BOILER PRESSURE: 12kg/cm²
SUPERHEATED (FOR CLASS 25d)

NORWAY 2–6–2T 1435mm

No 288 Class 32a [P. R-W

No 288, Class 32a is a superheated 2–6–2 Side Tank locomotive with out-side cylinders which is being preserved by the Norwegian Railway Club (*Norske-Jernbanen-Klub*). It was built in 1915 by Hamar (works number 101).

The NSB used 2–6–2 Side Tank locomotives extensively for its suburban services some of which (Class 32c) were built for the *Hoved Jernbane* by Baldwin and had bar frames. Others were built in 1915 for the *Bergen-banen* and for the *Solorbanen* (Class 32b): in 1919 some other sections of NSB received engines of Class 32c.

Classes 32a and 32b had plate frames. The piston valves were driven by Walschaerts valve gear; the boilers had round-top fireboxes and the heating surfaces varied between the sub-classes. The steam dome, with safety valves on top, was in the same casing, in front of the sand dome.

Dimensions: CYLINDERS: 525 × 600mm
COUPLED WHEELS: 1600mm
GRATE AREA: 1.90m²
BOILER PRESSURE: 12kg/cm²
SUPERHEATED

Narrow Gauge Steam Locomotive Preservation in Norway

There are, in Norway, several railway clubs and societies which own steam locomotives and which have taken over sections of track on which to run them.

The *Setesdalsbanen Hobbyklub*, Grovane owns four tank locomotives at least one of which is operated occasionally over 9km of 1067mm-gauge track between Grovane and Beiholen. This is part of the former NSB narrow gauge line which extended from Kristianstad 3km north of Kristiansand, due north, 58km to Bygglandsfjord.

Another narrow gauge (750mm) line is occasionally operated by *A/L Hölandsbanen*, Sorumsand over the former Urskog-Holandsbanen line of NSB.

NORWAY 4–4–0 1067mm

No 7 Class XIII is a two-cylinder compound 4–4–0 with outside cylinders which was built in 1901 by Thunes for the Jaeder Railways (*Jaederbanen*) which became part of the NSB.

This locomotive was the first to be built by the Norwegian firm of Thunes and it carries their works number 1.

It is preserved in the Railway Museum at Hamar.

Dimensions: CYLINDERS: HIGH PRESSURE: 320 × 457mm
LOW PRESSURE: 479 × 457mm
COUPLED WHEELS: 1397mm
GRATE AREA: 0.79m²
BOILER PRESSURE: 12kg/cm²

Sulitjelma Railway No 1 LOKE   [Brian Garvin

Sulitjelma Railway No 1 *LOKE* is an outside-cylinder 0–4–0 Side Tank locomotive with outside Allan link motion. It was built in 1892 by Hanomag (works number 2411) and is preserved in the Railway Museum at Hamar.

LOKE was built for the original 750mm gauge of the railway and assisted in the construction of the line which was opened in 1896. It was converted to 1067mm gauge in 1915 when the whole of the privately owned Sulitjelma Railway was also converted.

The railway, which serves iron ore mines, extends 36km from Lomi to Finneid near to Fauske on the main NSB line to Bodo and within the Arctic Circle. It remains privately owned and is now entirely diesel operated.

Dimensions: CYLINDERS: 279×457mm
              COUPLED WHEELS: 750mm
              GRATE AREA: 0.7m^2
              BOILER PRESSURE: 10kg/cm^2

Hamar-Grundset Railway No 21 ALF

[NSB Museum

No 21 *ALF* Class III is a 2–4–0 Side Tank locomotive built in 1870 as No 4 for the Hamar-Grundset Railway by Beyer, Peacock (works number 992). It has been restored to its original condition with spark-arresting chimney and it is preserved in the Railway Museum at Hamar.

The railway to the north, from Hamar to Støren and Trondheim via Roros, runs parallel to and to the east of the Hamar-Dombas-Trondheim line (the Dovre Line) which it joins at Støren. It was built to a gauge of 1067mm, completed in 1880 and was completely converted to 1435mm gauge, only in 1942, long after the completion of the 1435mm-gauge Dovre Line in 1921. Until 1921, journeys between Oslo and Trondheim had to be made via the Roros line and they involved a change of trains at Hamar due to the break of gauge there.

The first section of the Roros line, from Hamar to Elverum and Grundset, was privately built and it was for this railway that *ALF* was supplied.

Dimensions: CYLINDERS: 240 × 381mm
COUPLED WHEELS: 1143mm
GRATE AREA: 0.4m²
BOILER PRESSURE: 9.1kg/cm²

NSB No 6 Class XXII   [D. Pollard

NSB No 6 Class XXII is an outside-cylinder 2–4–2T built in 1902 by Thunes (works number 7) for the Kristianstad-Bygglandsfjord line of NSB. It is now owned by *Setesdalsbanen Hobbyklub* and it is stored at Grovane.

Dimensions: CYLINDERS: 279 × 457mm
                COUPLED WHEELS: 1146mm
                GRATE AREA: 0.7m^2
                BOILER PRESSURE: 10kg/cm^2

NSB No 2 Class XXI

[R. N. Joanes

NSB Nos 1, 2 and 5 of Class XXI are outside-cylinder 2–6–2 Side Tank locomotives which were used for working the line between Kristianstad and Bygglandsfjord (see page 76). They have short side tanks and spark arresting chimneys and are now fitted with Westinghouse brakes, the air reservoirs being carried on either side of the boiler. Outside Walschaerts valve gear operates slide valves above the cylinders.

These locomotives were built as under:

No 1 Dübs   works number 3172 of 1895
No 2 Dübs   works number 3173 of 1895
No 5 Thunes   works number 4 of 1902

These locomotives are now the property of the *Setesdalsbanen Hobbyklub*. No 1 is preserved and is on exhibition at Grovane Station. No 5 is in store and No 2 is used from time to time on the Club's track between Grovane and Beiholen, part of the original line.

Dimensions: CYLINDERS: 279 × 457mm
            COUPLED WHEELS: 914mm
            GRATE AREA: 0.7m^2
            BOILER PRESSURE: 10kg/cm^2

No 80 which is the same class as No 81 preserved   [NSB Museum

No 81 Class XXVI is an outside-cylinder 2–6–4 Back Tank locomotive built in 1914 by Hamar (works number 98). It worked on the Støren-Aamot section of the NSB and is now preserved in the Railway Museum at Hamar.

Dimensions: CYLINDERS: 375 × 460mm
COUPLED WHEELS: 1150mm
GRATE AREA: 0.86m²
BOILER PRESSURE: 12kg/cm²

No 2 URSKOG Class XXVII

[Brian Garvin

Urskog-Hölands Railway No 2 *URSKOG* Class XXVII is an outside-cylinder 0–6–0 Side Tank locomotive with outside Allan link motion and with a spark-arresting chimney. It was built in 1895 by Chemnitz (works number 2102); it is now preserved in the Railway Museum at Hamar.

The Urskog-Hölands Railway extended from Sørumsand, 56km south east to Skulerud, the whole railway being east of Oslo and near to the Swedish frontier. It was closed in 1959 but part of the line 2.7km long is now operated by *A/L Hölandsbanen*, Sørumsand and known as the Tertitten Railway.

Dimensions: CYLINDERS: 250 × 380mm
COUPLED WHEELS: 750mm
GRATE AREA: 0.5m²
BOILER PRESSURE: 12kg/cm²

No 4 SETSKOGEN Class XXVIII   [Brian Garvin

Urskog-Hölands Railway No 4 *SETSKOGEN* Class XXVIII is a 2–6–2 Side Tank locomotive with slide valves and outside Walschaerts valve gear built in 1909 by Chemnitz (works number 3356) and which is now the property of *A/L Hölandsbanen*, Sørumsand.

Dimensions: CYLINDERS: 260 × 400mm
             COUPLED WHEELS: 814mm
             GRATE AREA: 0.67m²
             BOILER PRESSURE: 12kg/cm²

Urskog-Hölands Railway No 7 *PRYDZ* Class XXIXb is an outside-cylinder 2–6–2 Side Tank locomotive built in 1950 by Henschel (works number 28463) and now preserved in working order in the Railway Museum at Hamar. This is a modern narrow-gauge tank engine with piston valves and outside Walschaerts valve gear.

Dimensions: CYLINDERS: 260 × 400mm
             COUPLED WHEELS: 824mm
             GRATE AREA: 0.67m²
             BOILER PRESSURE: 12kg/cm²
             SUPERHEATED

Urskog-Hölands Railway No 5 *BJORKELANGEN* Class XXIXa was built in 1924 by Chemnitz (works number 4623). It is now preserved in the Technical School at Trondheim.

Urskog-Hölands Railway No 6 *HÖLAND* Class XXIXa was built in 1925 by Chemnitz (works number 4658). This locomotive is now owned by *A/L Hölandsbanen*, Sørumsand (see page 76).

These two locomotives of Class XXIXa are superheated 2–6–2 Side Tank locomotives with outside cylinders and, in dimensions, identical with the later No 7 of Class XXIXb described above, except that the cylinders of Nos 5 and 6 are of greater diameter—280mm.

The Portuguese Railway Company

Until 1927 about half of the broad-gauge lines in Portugal were owned and operated by the *Companhia do Caminhos de Ferro Portugueses* (CP), a company largely financed in France, which had been formed in 1860 and had built the main Lisbon-Oporto line. Most of the other lines were state-owned, the most important being the *Sul e Sueste* (SS) south of the Tagus, and the *Minho e Douro* (MD) to the north and east of Oporto. This latter railway had also a considerable mileage of metre gauge feeder lines running down the valleys to the Douro line. There were several other independent metre-gauge lines, as well as the important broad gauge *Beira Alta*.

On May 11, 1927, the CP obtained a lease to operate all the state-owned railways, both broad and metre gauge, but a year later the CP leased its metre gauge lines to two independent railways, the Northern of Portugal and the National Railways Company. In 1948, however, the CP obtained a concession to lease all the broad and metre gauge lines, including the *Beira Alta* and the metre gauge *Vale do Vouga*, and now it operates all the Portuguese railways with the single exception of the short electrified Estoril Railway, which still retains its independence.

Steam Locomotive Preservation in Portugal

At the present time it is known that three 1665mm-gauge steam locomotives will be preserved and that two others, both o–4–o Well Tank shunting locomotives, are probably to be preserved. There is at present, no indication that any 1000mm gauge engines will be kept.

The site of the future Railway Museum has not yet been decided.

PORTUGAL 2–2–2 1665mm

D. LUIZ as built

[Beyer Peacock

No 01 *D. LUIZ* is a 2–2–2 locomotive built in 1862 by Beyer, Peacock for the South Eastern Railway of Portugal and exhibited at the London Exposition of that year. It was one of the largest "single wheelers" ever to be built for the broad gauge and it was withdrawn only in 1934. It has now been restored to its original condition and is in store at the Estremoz Depot of the CP.

The locomotive, when built, was domeless and without a cab. The sand-boxes were below the running plates. During its working life, it received a small sand dome on the second ring of the boiler and a corrugated iron cab roof. At the time of World War I, the Portuguese Railways were short of coal and a lot of their locomotives were converted to burn wood. *D. LUIZ*, and many others, were then fitted with large and ugly spark arresting chimneys which were retained until the mid-1920s.

Dimensions: CYLINDERS: 406 × 558mm
DRIVING WHEELS: 2133mm
GRATE AREA: 1.6m²
BOILER PRESSURE: 9kg/cm²

2–4–0 No 9

[Brian Garvin

No 9 is an outside-cylinder 2–4–0 locomotive built in 1875 by Beyer, Peacock for the Minho and Douro Railway on which railway it was also No 9.

It is at present stored at Braga Locomotive Depot and will be preserved.

Ten locomotives, Nos 1–10, were delivered to the Minho and Douro between 1872 and 1878, but only seven survived to come into CP ownership. They were handsome and long-lived machines. They had polished brass domes surmounted by Salter safety valves (later removed) and copper-topped chimneys. Ugly square sandboxes (standard Minho and Douro practice) were mounted on the boilers between chimney and dome. They were built for working on the Campanhia-Minho line on which their passenger-train load was 120 tonnes.

Dimensions: CYLINDERS: 420 × 560mm
COUPLED WHEELS: 1600mm
GRATE AREA: 1.5m²
BOILER PRESSURE: 8kg/cm²

2–2–2ST No 02049 is awaiting preservation at Braga

No 02049 is an inside-cylinder 2–2–2 Saddle Tank locomotive which was built in 1854 by Fairbairn of Leeds. It was purchased, second-hand, by the Minho and Douro Railway for the opening of that railway in 1874 and became their No 13.

The boiler had a large dome, surmounted by Salter safety valves, over the firebox and a large Minho and Douro standard type square sandbox was mounted on the saddle tank above the driving wheels. A cab roof with ornamental iron side-brackets, was provided after the engine came to Portugal.

During the early years of this century, No 13 was used for working light passenger trains, not exceeding 60 tonnes, between Campanhia and Oporto Central Station.

No 13 as CP No 02049 is now stored at Braga Locomotive Depot and is to be preserved.

Dimensions: CYLINDERS: 306 × 458mm
DRIVING WHEELS: 1525mm
BOILER PRESSURE: 8 atm
WEIGHT (W.O.): 28.75 tonnes

o–4–oWT № oo2   [R. G. Farr

Nos 001, 002 and 003 are small outside-cylinder 0–4–0 Well Tank loco-motives of which four were built for the CP and which have retained their original numbers. They have slide valves operated by outside Allan link motion. Their duties were as shed pilots and for shunting around industrial premises.

It is believed that one of the engines will be preserved but there are three at present in store and these may occasionally be in use.

No 001 was built in 1881 by Chemnitz (works number 1132) and is at Abrantes depot. No 002 also built in 1881 by Chemnitz (works number 1133) is at Vila Nova de Gaia. No 003 was built in 1890 by Cockerill (works number 1601) and is at present at Oporto—Contumil Depot.

Dimensions: CYLINDERS: 225 × 400mm
                 COUPLED WHEELS: 800mm
                 GRATE AREA: 0.6m^2
                 BOILER PRESSURE: 10kg/cm^2

0–4–0WT No 005   [P. R-W

No 005 is an outside-cylinder 0–4–0 Well Tank locomotive with a vertical boiler. It was built for CP in 1901 by Cockerill (works number 2342) and is at present stored at Abrantes Depot and will be preserved.

This locomotive has outside Walschaerts valve gear and a Detroit lubricator is fitted for cylinder lubrication. The *raison d'être* of this locomotive is not known. It was the only one of its class.

Dimensions: CYLINDERS: 250 × 260mm
COUPLED WHEELS: 615mm
GRATE AREA: 0.83m²
BOILER PRESSURE: 10kg/cm²

Spanish National Railway System

The broad, 1674mm-gauge railways of Spain were nationalised in 1941 by the formation of *Red Nacional de los Ferrocarriles Españoles* (RENFE) which amalgamated the five principal companies, Madrid-Zaragoza-Alicante (MZA), Northern (*Norte*), Andaluces, Central of Aragon and National Western (*Oeste*). Many smaller companies were also included in RENFE but none of the numerous narrow-gauge companies was nationalised though some are operated on behalf of the State by an organisation known as FEVE.

Steam Locomotive Preservation in Spain

Spain has a rich heritage of steam locomotives from which to choose a representative selection for a Railway Museum. Nearly every type of locomotive has, at some time, seen service on the 1674mm-gauge lines and nearly every form of blast-pipe, feed pump, lubricator and auxiliary equipment has been in use.

There has been, for some years, a small Railway Museum owned by RENFE at San Cosme y San Damian, 1 Madrid, and this houses one small locomotive and some excellent models. As in so many countries, the need exists for a railway museum in which there is sufficient space to preserve a reasonable number of full-size locomotives which show the essential development of the steam locomotive in Spain. The Spanish Government has indicated that such a museum will be provided, but the location has not been decided. As a result, and until the space to be available is known, a considerable number of withdrawn locomotives has been stored in various depots up and down the country. An effort is now being made to concentrate those which are "scheduled for preservation" at the old steam shed at Clot, Barcelona (known as the *Museum Talleres Generales de Clot*) and at the depot at Cuenca in Alcazar de San Juan.

It is by no means certain that all the locomotives stored will be found space in the Railway Museum.

Largely through the good offices of Don Gustavo Reder, representatives of several important types, some of them still at work, may be preserved.

The following documentation shows those locomotives for which preservation is certain together with others which will probably go to the Railway Museum. The list is presented in the usual order of wheel arrangements and the number given at the commencement of each section is that given to the locomotive by RENFE. It is likely that, on restoration, the original companies' numbers and liveries will be used.

Preservation by private individuals in Spain is rare and there are few broad-gauge engines on display in public places. Those which are so preserved are included in the list and their locations are indicated.

Full-scale working replica of No 1 MATARO   [P. R-W

No 1 *MATARO* is a full-scale working replica of one of the first four loco-motives in Spain. It was built in 1948 by La Maquinista (works number 649) for the Centenary celebrations of the first railway in Spain which was opened for traffic on October 28, 1848. This railway was constructed with British capital and extended 28.2km from Barcelona northwards along the coast, to Mataro. The gauge was 1674mm. It ultimately became part of the Tarragona, Barcelona and France Railway and later of the Madrid-Zaragoza-Alicante Railway.

Four 2–2–2 outside-cylinder locomotives were constructed for the railway by Messrs. Jones and Potts of Newton-le-Willows, Lancashire, England and they carried the names *MATARO, BARCELONA, CATA-LUÑA* and *BESOS*. They were of the well-known "Allan" or "Crewe" design, and were almost identical with engines built by the same firm at the same time for the London and Blackwall Railway. The dimensions of the Spanish engines were:

CYLINDERS: 350 × 500mm
DRIVING WHEELS: 1524mm
BOILER PRESSURE: 6kg/cm^2

The replica Mataró *with a train of the period is at present stored at Cuenca.*

No 120.2131 which is preserved   [P. R-W

No 120.2131 is an outside cylinder 2–4–0 built as No 7 for the Salamanca-Portuguese Frontier Railway in 1884 by Esslingen (works number 2042). Thirteen of these engines were built and No 7 became No 77 of the National Western Railway (*Oeste*) which took over the Salamanca and Portuguese Frontier in 1928. It is at present in store at Alcaniz and is scheduled for possible preservation in the Railway Museum.

Dimensions: CYLINDERS: 440 × 680mm

                COUPLED WHEELS: 1450mm

                GRATE AREA: 2.1m^2

                BOILER PRESSURE: 9kg/cm^2

No 220.2005 as it appeared before restoration

[P. R-W

No 220.2005 was built by Hartmann in 1881 (works number 1122) for the *Real Compania Portguesa* as their No 9. This company became the Madrid, Cáceres and Portugal Railway which in turn became part of the amalgamation which formed the National Western Railway (*Oeste*). Five of these inside cylinder 4–4–0s were built and all came into the stock of RENFE in 1941. No 9 was then renumbered to 220.2005 and, after being withdrawn in 1960, is now in the *Museum Taleres Generales de Clot* at Barcelona.

Dimensions: CYLINDERS: 462 × 610mm
            COUPLED WHEELS: 1860mm
            GRATE AREA: 2.3m^2
            BOILER PRESSURE: 9kg/cm^2

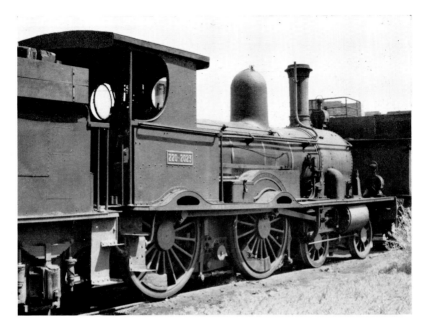

[P. R-W

No 220.2023 is a very English-looking outside-cylinder 4–4–0 built in 1891 by Beyer, Peacock (works number 3356) and which is at present at Alicante Termino in store for the future Railway Museum.

It was originally Algeciras-Bobadilla Railway No 6 *BOBADILLA* and was one of three built in the same year for working over the mountainous main line of that Company. Two further engines of the same design, apart from having higher boiler pressure and smaller coupled wheels (1600mm), were supplied to the Company in 1912.

The Andaluces Railway bought the Algeciras-Bobadilla in 1913 but these old engines were kept on their original duties until 1926 when they were transferred to Alicante.

In 1941, the three original engines, Nos 4, 5 and 6 became RENFE Nos 220.2021, 2022 and 2023 respectively.

Dimensions: CYLINDERS: 457 × 609mm
        COUPLED WHEELS: 1714mm
        GRATE AREA: 1.9m^2
        BOILER PRESSURE: 9.8kg/cm^2

No 030.2016 was a sister engine to the preserved No 030.2013   [P. R-W

Inside-cylinder 0–6–0 No 030.2013 was built as No 246 for the Madrid-Zaragosa-Alicante Railway (MZA) by Ritson, Wilson at Leeds in 1857 (works number 607). It is in the *Museum Talleres Generales de Clot*, Barcelona.

Seventy of these engines were built for the MZA, the first ten by Ritson, Wilson in 1857, 17 by Kitsons in 1857–58 and the remainder by Cail in 1858. They were a very long-lived class, many of them being in service for over 100 years and apart from being given better cabs, they were little changed during their long lives.

Dimensions: CYLINDERS: 440 × 600mm
COUPLED WHEELS: 1430mm
GRATE AREA: 1.3m²
BOILER PRESSURE: 8kg/cm²

No 030.2107 EL ALAGON when in service as shed pilot at Delicias [P. R-W

No 030.2107 *EL ALAGON* is an old outside-cylinder o–6–o with outside Stephenson Link motion operating slide valves above the cylinders. It is at present stored at Cuenca and will probably go to the Railway Museum.

This engine was built as a 2–4–o for the Northern Railway (*Norte*) by Ateliers d'Oullins in 1861, works number 306. It was first numbered 127 in the *Norte* list but this was changed to 382 and again to 1382 before it was sold, in 1873, to the Medina del Campo-Salamanca Railway as their No 9. It was rebuilt as an o–6–o in 1877 and when its parent company was amalgamated with the National Western Railway (*Oeste*) in 1928, it became *Oeste* No 119. It ended its days as RENFE 030.2107 at Madrid, Delicias, Depot as a mobile boiler washing out plant.

Dimenisons: CYLINDERS: 400 × 600mm
　　　　　　COUPLED WHEELS: 1300mm
　　　　　　GRATE AREA: 1.3m²
　　　　　　BOILER PRESSURE: 8kg/cm²

No 030.2110 *PERRUCA* may be preserved for the Railway Museum and is said to be in store at Villanueva y Geltru. It was built by André Koechlin (later to become part of Société Alsacienne) in 1870 for the Memphis, El Paso and Pacific Railway. Ten such locomotives were built but, as the railway concerned became bankrupt, they never reached North America and five were purchased by various Spanish railways, *PERRUCA* going to the Asturias, Galicia and León Railway which was taken over by the Northern Railway (*Norte*) in 1890. *PERRUCA* became *Norte* No 1653. It has outside Gooch valve gear and outside steam pipes.

As built, these locomotives were wood-burners and a large spark arresting chimney was fitted together with high rails round the top of the tender. Three side windows in each side of the cab and a long protruding cow-catcher were the only other apparent "Americanisms", the basic design being essentially French. They were to be numbered 1 to 10 on the Memphis, El Paso and Pacific and the works numbers were 1253 to 1262 respectively. All of them were to be named after North American rivers, but probably only No 1 *MISSISSIPPI RIVER* and No 2 *WHITE RIVER* ever carried their names.

Dimensions: CYLINDERS: 460 × 650mm
COUPLED WHEELS: 1520mm
GRATE AREA: 1.6m²
BOILER PRESSURE: 8kg/cm²

MZA No 413 was a sister engine of RENFE No 030.2216   [RENFE

No 030.2216 is an outside-cylinder 0–6–0 which was one of 14 such locomotives built for the Madrid, Ciudad Real and Badajoz Railway. It was, briefly, No 58 of that company having been built in 1880 by Fives Lille (works number 2272). The Madrid-Zaragoza-Alicante (MZA) took over No 58 and its owning company in 1880 and the engine became MZA No 408.

Salter safety valves surmount the rather large dome and the main steam pipes leave the boiler immediately behind the chimney. The valve gear is inside Stephenson link motion.

No 030.2216 is at present stored at Alcázar-de-San-Juan but it is shortly to be placed on display in the public gardens in that town.

Dimensions: CYLINDERS: 450 × 650mm
COUPLED WHEELS: 1420mm
GRATE AREA: 2.0m²
BOILER PRESSURE: 8.5kg/cm²

No 030.2230 when in service [P. R-W

No 030.2230 is an inside-cylinder 0–6–0 which was built for the Almansa, Valencia and Tarragona Railway as their No 85 by Sharp Stewart in 1891, works number 3687. Eight such locomotives were supplied and they had inside Allan link motion.

When this 117km-long railway was taken over by the Northern Railway (Norte) in 1901, No 85 became Norte No 1726 and later, in RENFE ownership, it spent many years at Sagunto. It was on display at Valencia Termino Station but has been removed and stored in Valencia Alameda Depot. Its future is uncertain.

Dimensions: CYLINDERS: 483 × 660mm
COUPLED WHEELS: 1524mm
GRATE AREA: 2.0m²
BOILER PRESSURE: 8kg/cm²

No 030.2332 which was almost identical with the preserved locomotive No 030.2264   [P. R-W

No 030.2264 is an old outside-cylinder 0–6–0 with inside Stephenson link motion. It is stored at Cuenca and will probably be preserved. This engine was Madrid-Zaragosa-Alicante No 204 (Schneider 563/1861) and was one of 43 which were built by Schneider and by Graffenstaden between 1861 and 1864. Many of them saw more than a century of service and, apart from the provision of bigger cabs, they were little altered.

Dimensions: CYLINDERS: 450 × 650mm
COUPLED WHEELS: 1310mm
GRATE AREA: 1.5m²
BOILER PRESSURE: 8kg/cm²

No 030.2369 which is preserved [R. G. Farr

No 030.2369 was built in 1884 by Sharp Stewart (works number 3212) as No 4 of the Alcantarilla to Lorca Railway. It was one of six which were the only locomotives owned by the railway.

With inside cylinders, Ramsbottom safety valves and a shapely tapered chimney these engines were of obvious British ancestry and indeed were very similar in appearance and dimensions to many contemporary British locomotives. No 030.2369 is now at Lorca and will be preserved in the Railway Museum.

Dimensions: CYLINDERS: 457×610mm
COUPLED WHEELS: 1375mm
GRATE AREA: 1.9m^2
BOILER PRESSURE: 9kg/cm^2

No 030.2472, a sister engine to the preserved No 030.2471. The view shows the engine at work on a train from Valencia to Caudiel   [P. R-W

No 030.2471 is at Valencia Alameda Depot awaiting preservation in the Railway Museum. This was Central of Aragon Railway No 1 (Couillet 1279/01), the first of a batch of eight identical locomotives to be supplied in 1901 by this Belgian builder. They were powerful machines with comparatively large coupled wheels which made them very suitable for passenger train duties on this heavily graded main line.

They had two sets of Walschaerts valve gear with eccentrics, eccentric rods and expansion links inside the frames but with the union links, combination levers and radius rods outside and deriving their motion from the crossheads. The two motions were combined through rocking shafts.

Dimensions: CYLINDERS: 480 × 600mm
COUPLED WHEELS: 1700mm
GRATE AREA: 3.0m^2
BOILER PRESSURE: 12kg/cm^2

No 130.2140 JARAVIA which was identical with the preserved locomotive   [P. R-W

No 130.2124 *AGUILAS* was built by Neilson (works number 3846) in 1889 for the Great Southern of Spain Railway which had been constructed with British capital. The makers' plates with the name of the owning company in English is affixed to the cab sides. Twenty-five of these very British-looking 2–6–os were built by Neilson (12), Kitson (2), Sharp Stewart (5) and North British (6) between the years 1889 and 1905.

The Great Southern main line was between three towns and the company changed its name to the *FC de Lorca a Baza y Aguilas* in 1922 but the numbers 1–25, of the locomotives remained until the formation of RENFE in 1941.

No 130.2124 is at present stored at Aguilas and will eventually be put on display in the gardens of that town.

Dimensions: CYLINDERS: 457 × 609mm
            COUPLED WHEELS: 1447mm
            GRATE AREA: 2.2m^2
            BOILER PRESSURE: 15kg/cm^2

No 230.2051 which was identical with the preserved locomotive   [P. R-W

No 230.2059 is at present in store at the sub depot at Logroño and it will eventually go to the Railway Museum.

This is another very British-looking locomotive with Belpaire firebox, Ramsbottom safety valves and with outside Walschaerts valve gear operating slide valves above the cylinders. It was built by the North British Locomotive Company (works number 17647) in 1907 for the Beira-Alta Railway of Portugal and was one of three which were built in 1907 followed by another three in 1909. All six engines were later sold to the Medina del Campo-Zamora-Orense and Vigo Railway of Spain which numbered them 60–65 inclusive.

On September 8, 1928 this company formed one of the constituents of the new National Western Railway (*Oeste*) and with their third change of ownership the six 4–6–0s became Nos 760–765. Finally they all came into RENFE ownership as 230.2059–2064.

Dimensions: CYLINDERS: 483 × 600mm
           COUPLED WHEELS: 1562mm
           GRATE AREA: 2.5m^2
           BOILER PRESSURE: 12kg/cm^2

No 230.2098 of the same class as the preserved No 230.2085 [P. R-W

No 230.2085 was built for the Northern Railway of Spain (*Norte*) as their No 3101 in 1910 by the Société Hannoverienne (works number 5943). It is at present stored at Valencia, Alameda Depot and will be put on display in the Railway Museum.

This is one of 60 very successful superheated 4–6–0 locomotives with piston valves and Walschaerts valve gear. They might be said to be the *Norte* equivalent of the Prussian P8 or the British Railways Class 5. In 1904, the same builders had delivered to the *Norte*, 30 slightly smaller engines with slide valves and using saturated steam and ten of these were later superheated and provided with larger piston valve cylinders, making them equivalent to the 1909 engines.

Dimensions: CYLINDERS: 500×650mm
COUPLED WHEELS: 1750mm
GRATE AREA: 2.7m^2
BOILER PRESSURE: 12kg/cm^2
SUPERHEATED

MZA No 656 which was identical with RENFE No 230.4001 preserved   [RENFE

No 230.4001 is a four-cylinder compound 4–6–0 with high pressure cylinders outside the frames driving the middle coupled wheels and the low pressure cylinders between the frames driving the leading coupled axle. The inside cylinders are, therefore, placed well in advance of those outside. The valve gear is Walschaerts and the cut-off is independent for high pressure and low pressure cylinders.

This locomotive was built in 1901 as No 651 for the Madrid-Zaragosa-Alicante Railway (MZA) by the Société Hannoverienne and was their works number 3654. The builders supplied 15 of these engines to the MZA in 1901, all with slide valves. A further 15 were supplied by Henschel in 1903 and these had piston valves.

No 230.4001 is at present at the *Museum Talleres Generales de Clot* in Barcelona.

Dimensions: CYLINDERS: HIGH PRESSURE: 350 × 650mm
LOW PRESSURE: 550 × 650mm
COUPLED WHEELS: 1750mm
GRATE AREA: 2.7m^2
BOILER PRESSURE: 14kg/cm^2

SPAIN · 0–8–0 · 1674mm

No 040.2116 EL ULRON which was a sister engine to EL CINCA [P. R-W

040.2091 *EL CINCA* was built as No 2501 for the Northern Railway (*Norte*) in 1863 by Schneider (works number 717). It was the first 0–8–0 to run on the 1674mm gauge in Spain and the design followed closely that of similar engines built for the French *Chemin de Fer du Midi*. Thirty-seven of the class were built by Schneider of Creusot between 1863 and 1866 and all survived to come into the stock of RENFE in 1941, most of them working on to become centenarians. All carried names except RENFE No 040.2115.

Outside Stephenson link motion operated slide valves above the cylinders. The very large dome on the first ring of the boiler was surmounted by Salter safety valves. All the engines had four-wheeled tenders.

No 040.2091 is probably for preservation and display in the Railway Museum. It is at present at Cuenca.

Dimensions: CYLINDERS: 500 × 660mm
COUPLED WHEELS: 1300mm
GRATE AREA: 1.9m²
BOILER PRESSURE: 9kg/cm²

No 040.2273 was No 549 of the Madrid-Zaragoza-Alicante Railway (MZA), an outside cylinder 0–8–0 with slide valves above the cylinders angled outwards at about 15 deg and operated by Walschaerts valve gear. It was one of the early engines to be built by the famous Barcelona locomotive builders La Maquinista Terrestre y Maritima and was their

107

MZA No 550 which was identical with RENFE No 040.2273 preserved [RENFE

works number 20 of 1900. Fifteen of these engines were built for main line freight duties on the MZA.

No 040.2273 is at present at Seville, San Jeronimo Depot and is to be preserved in the Railway Museum.

Dimensions: CYLINDERS: 500 × 650mm
        COUPLED WHEELS: 1304mm
        GRATE AREA: 2.6m²
        BOILER PRESSURE: 10.5kg/cm²

No 040.2082 is an outside-cylinder 0–8–0 freight locomotive which was built in 1865 by Avonside (works number 586) for the Zaragoza-Barcelona Railway, as their No 102. It was taken over by the Northern Railway (*Norte*) in 1878 and became No 2582 of that system. It is now in store at Logroño and is scheduled for preservation in the Railway Museum.

Twelve of these engines were built by Avonside in 1865 and a further eight by Schneider in 1877. They all had Stephenson link motion operating slide valves, both being inside the frames. The British-built engines had round-section connecting and coupling rods. All had Belpaire boilers and the large dome was surmounted by Salter safety valves.

Dimensions: CYLINDERS: 505 × 610mm
        COUPLED WHEELS: 1295mm
        GRATE AREA: 2.34m²
        BOILER PRESSURE: 9kg/cm²

No 141.2002, an identical engine to that which is preserved   [P. R-W

No 141.2001 is the first of 52 locomotives of the 2–8–2 type built for the Northern Railway (*Norte*) during 1917 and 1918 by the American Locomotive Company of Schenectady (ALCO). It was *Norte* No 4501 and it carries the ALCO works number 56671.

During the last years of World War I and for several years after, the European locomotive industry was very fully occupied and its products were very expensive. Many railways, therefore, turned to the United States for motive power and locomotives were supplied which, apart from details, were built to American standard practice—bar frames, wide steel fireboxes with radial stays, grease lubrication and, as in the *Norte* engines, mellow, deep-toned whistles.

No 141.2001 is at present stored at Seville, San Jeronimo, Depot and will ultimately go to the Railway Museum.

Dimensions: CYLINDERS: 570 × 710mm
COUPLED WHEELS: 1560mm
GRATE AREA: 4.1m^2
BOILER PRESSURE: 12.7kg/cm^2
SUPERHEATED

No 141.2280, one of the class of modern Mikados of which one will be preserved   [P. R-W

One of the numerous RENFE standard 2–8–2 locomotives will be preserved in the Railway Museum. Many are still in service and it is not yet known which engine will be kept.

Between 1953 and 1960, 242 of these very successful mixed traffic Mikados were built, most by the four Spanish builders—La Maquinista, Euskalduna, Babcock & Wilcox and Macosa. The North British Locomotive Company built 25 of the first order for 125 engines, and also provided much finished material to the Spanish builders.

The engines vary in detail. Some were built as coal burners with single Kylala blast pipes; later engines burned oil fuel and had double Kylchap blast pipes, and some of the earlier engines were converted to oil firing while retaining their single chimneys. Two have been given Giesl ejectors and a few had ACFI water pumps and heaters. Early engines had the sand dome and steam dome under a single cover but a large saddle shaped sandbox sits on the boilers of later engines. Walschaerts valve gear operates piston valves and the leading and trailing pony truck axles have roller bearings.

Dimensions: CYLINDERS: 570 × 710mm
               COUPLED WHEELS: 1560mm
               GRATE AREA: 4.8m²
               BOILER PRESSURE: 15kg/cm²
               SUPERHEATED

No 240.2174 which was identical with the preserved locomotive No 240.2081
[Lawrence Marshall

No 240.2081 was No 1101 of the Madrid-Zaragoza-Alicante Railway (MZA) and was built in 1912 by Henschel (works number 11526). It is probable that this engine, the first of its type on the MZA, will be exhibited in the Railway Museum and it is at present in store at Seville, San Jeronimo Depot.

Another locomotive of the same class is in store at the *Museum Talleres Generales de Clot*, Barcelona. This is RENFE No 240.2135, MZA No 1155, Henschel 12122/13 and this locomotive is probably an alternative choice for preservation.

The 4–8–0 became a very popular type in Spain for both freight and mixed traffic duties and from 1912 until 1953 many hundreds were built; all the major broad gauge railways used the type. The MZA had 120 of its first class of 4–8–0 from Henschel, the last 25 being built in 1921 and the railway then ordered, from the same builder, another 165 of an improved class and suitable for express train working.

No 240.2081 and her sisters have Walschaerts valve gear, piston valves and can normally develop 1755 indicated horse-power.

Dimensions: CYLINDERS: 580 × 660mm

        COUPLED WHEELS: 1400mm

        GRATE AREA: 3.9m²

        BOILER PRESSURE: 12kg/cm²

        SUPERHEATED

No 240.4041 which was of the same class as No 240.4001 preserved [R. G. Farr

No 240.4001 is a four-cylinder de Glehn compound 4–8–0 which was No 4001 of the Northern Railway (*Norte*). It was built by the Société Alsacienne and was their works number 6278 of 1912. Twenty engines were built by the same firm in 1912-14 and Henschel delivered another 25 in 1921. No 240.4001 is at Cuenca and is scheduled for preservation in the Railway Museum.

The 4001 Class of the *Norte* were actually the first (by a few weeks) main line 4–8–0s in Spain and were completely different machines from the contemporary MZA engines (qv). They were, of course, essentially French in design and were an obvious development of the four-cylinder de Glehn compound Pacifics which were introduced on the *Norte* in 1911. Many of both types were fitted with the ugly and cumbersome Worthington feed water pump on the Right hand side of the engine but some had Dabeg pumps which, at least, are less unsightly.

Dimensions: CYLINDERS: HIGH PRESSURE: 400 × 640mm
                          LOW PRESSURE: 620 × 640mm
        COUPLED WHEELS: 1560mm
        GRATE AREA: 4.1m²
        BOILER PRESSURE: 16kg/cm²
        SUPERHEATED

No 240.3008 is identical with the preserved locomotive [R. G. Farr

No 240.3001 is a three-cylinder 4–8–0 which was built as No 4301 for the Northern Railway (*Norte*) in 1922 by the Yorkshire Engine Company of Sheffield (works number 1658), who were sub-contracting for Babcock & Wilcox of Bilbao (works number 101).

The four-cylinder compound 4–8–0s of the *Norte* (qv) were excellent machines but, after ten years of service, more power was required and, following the current British trend for three-cylinder engines with conjugated valve gear, No 4301 and her 14 sisters were put to work on the mountainous main line of the *Norte* between Madrid and Avila and on to Venta de Baños. They were singularly unsuccessful and were frequently short of steam. They ended their comparatively short lives working coal trains in the Ponferrada area where No 4301 (as 240.3001) is now stored. It may be preserved as it is of interest in belonging to one of the only two classes of three-cylinder engines in Spain.

Dimensions: CYLINDERS (3): 520 × 660mm
        COUPLED WHEELS: 1560mm
        GRATE AREA: 4.6m²
        BOILER PRESSURE: 13kg/cm²
        SUPERHEATED

No 241.4060 which was the same class as No 241.4001 which may be preserved   [P. R-W

Apart from ten 4–8–4s, the ultimate express locomotives in Spain were 4–8–2s and there were some very fine examples of this type. In all, 256 of five different classes were built. As had happened previously with other types, the Northern Railway (*Norte*) first introduced the 4–8–2 in 1925, followed closely by the Madrid-Zaragoza-Alicante (MZA) later the same year and one example of each of these pioneer classes will probably be preserved in the Railway Museum.

No 241.4001 was No 4601 of the *Norte* and was built in 1925 by Hanomag (works number 10495). This engine is at present in store at León. It was the first of 66 locomotives which were built in batches between 1925 and 1930, the first six by Hanomag and the rest by the three Spanish builders La Maquinista, Euskalduna and Babcock & Wilcox.

It is a de Glehn-du Bousquet four-cylinder compound with the four cylinders in line, the high pressure outside, driving the second coupled axle and the low pressure cylinders, inside the frames, driving the leading coupled axle. The cut-off is independent for the high pressure and the low pressure cylinders.

The very large boiler has a combustion chamber and the original single blast pipe and small chimney was replaced by a Kylchap double blast pipe and double chimney in 1939. No 4601 and her sisters were excellent machines and of beautiful appearance. One of the class, No 4048, was rebuilt in 1939 with new cylinders, Dabeg o.c. poppet valves and Kylchap double exhaust to become the prototype for a series of modern 4–8–2s to be built for the RENFE.

Dimensions of No 4001 as built:

CYLINDERS: HIGH PRESSURE: 460 × 680mm

LOW PRESSURE: 700 × 680mm

COUPLED WHEELS: 1750mm

GRATE AREA: 5.0m²

BOILER PRESSURE: 16kg/cm²

SUPERHEATED

No 241.2058 which was of the same class as No 241.2001 which may be preserved   [P. R-W

One of the original MZA 4-8-2 locomotives will probably be preserved in the Railway Museum. It is not known which one will be chosen, but it will probably be No 241.2001 which was built in 1925 by La Maquinista (works number 179) as MZA No 1701. It was the first of the class and is now stored at Cuenca.

MZA Nos 1701-1795 were built by La Maquinista during the seven years 1925-1931. They were, in some respects, an enlarged express-engine version of the very successful "1400" Class 4-8-0s and they have proved to be equally as successful in their faster and heavier duties.

There were five distinct modifications of these engines in MZA days:

Nos 1756-1765 and 1776-1790 were oil burning.

Nos 1766-1775 and 1791-1795 had electric lighting (the remainder had acetylene gas lighting).

Nos 1770-1775 had Lentz o.c. poppet valves.

Nos 1776-1795 had Dabeg o.c. poppet valves (the remainder had piston valves).

Nos 1776-1795 had Dabeg feed water pumps and heaters.

The weights of these "sub classes" differed from one another. In RENFE ownership, most of the piston valve engines acquired double blast pipes and chimneys and some of the poppet valve engines had raised running plates above the cylinders.

Dimensions: CYLINDERS: 620 × 710mm   GRATE AREA: 4.9m²

COUPLED WHEELS: 1750mm   BOILER PRESSURE: 14kg/cm²

SUPERHEATED

115

No 151.3115 which was identical to No 151.5001   [P. R-W

No 151.3101 is a three-cylinder 2–10–2 heavy freight locomotive which was built for RENFE in 1942 by La Maquinista (works number 574). It is at present in store at Calatayud and will go, ultimately, to the Railway Museum.

Twenty-two of these large and powerful locomotives were built for RENFE by La Maquinista in the four years 1942–45. Originally numbered 151.5001–5022 they were renumbered and, for most of their lives, carried the numbers 151.3101–3122. Their original duties were working coal trains from the Ponferrada Mines to the coast at La Coruña but they later worked between Leon and Venta de Baños.

The three cylinders were in line, the inside cylinder driving the second coupled axle and the two outside, the third. Three sets of Walschaerts valve gear operated Lentz oscillating cam poppet valves and a double Kylchap blast pipe was provided. The leading axle formed a Krauss truck with the leading coupled axle.

The large round-top boilers were identical with those of the 4–8–2 locomotives of Series 241.2201–2257, and seven of the class were oil-burners. The engines were fitted with ACFI feed water pumps and heaters and they had, at one time, electric fans which were used when passing through tunnels to draw fresh air in at the front of the engine and exhaust it into the cab.

These locomotives were among the most powerful in Europe.

Dimensions: CYLINDERS (3): 570 × 750mm
COUPLED WHEELS: 1560mm
GRATE AREA: 5.3m²
BOILER PRESSURE: 16kg/cm²
SUPERHEATED

No 060.4014 which was an identical engine to No 060.4013 to be preserved   [P. R-W

No 060.4013 is to be preserved in the Railway Museum and is at present at Valencia Termino Depot. It is a four-cylinder Mallet compound articulated o–6–6–o which was built as No 53 for the Central of Aragon Railway in 1906. The builders of this and three other similar locomotives were Esslingen and their works number is 3359. They were, however, sub-contractors to the Swiss Locomotive Company whose works number is 1748 for this engine.

The Central of Aragon has perhaps the most difficult and mountainous main lines in Spain and from the early days of this century it used Mallet and, later, much more powerful Garratt articulated locomotives.

The first Mallet locomotives built for the railway were of the 2–6–6–0 type and were all scrapped many years ago. No 060.4013 is a representative of the second class of these Mallet engines with slide valves for both high pressure and low pressure cylinders using saturated steam.

Dimensions: CYLINDERS: HIGH PRESSURE: 400×600mm
                   LOW PRESSURE: 600×600mm

       COUPLED WHEELS: 1200mm
       GRATE AREA: 2.5m^2
       BOILER PRESSURE: 13kg/cm^2

No 3 is a 2–2–2 Side Tank locomotive built in 1864 for the Huesca-Tardienta Railway, a 21.7km line connecting the capital of Huesca Province, north of Zaragoza, with the *Norte* line from Zaragoza to Lerida at Tardienta. It later became the property of the Zaragoza-Barcelona Railway on which it was No 2T. This line was taken over by the Northern Railway (*Norte*) who, in 1910, sold the engine to the Azucarera Industrial Company. It became their No 3 and was used at their sugar factory at Aranda de Duero. No 3 was stored there until recently but is now in the locomotive depot at Madrid-Delicias. The Company have presented it to RENFE and it will be exhibited at Alcazar when it has been restored.

Dimensions: NOT KNOWN

Andaluces No 01 in the Railway Museum at Madrid   [RENFE

No 020.0201 has been restored and is on exhibition in the RENFE Museum in the Cal de San Cosme y San Damian, Madrid. It is the only "full size" exhibit in the museum. This rather diminutive 0–4–0 Well Tank locomotive now carries its previous number Andaluces Railway 01. It has outside Stephenson link motion and was built in 1871 for the 4km-long Jerez Urban Railway by Schneider, works number 1427; it was taken over with that railway, by the Andaluces in 1892.

For many years it worked a single-coach "train" to carry railwaymen between two passenger stations in Seville and the San Jeronimo Motive Power Depot where it was always referred to as the *ratón* (mouse).

Dimensions: CYLINDERS: 200 × 360mm
COUPLED WHEELS: 805mm
GRATE AREA: 0.4m²
BOILER PRESSURE: 8kg/cm²

No 020.0221 GALINDO

[RENFE

No 020.0221, *GALINDO*, originally belonged to the Triano Railway as their No 4 built by Sharp Stewart in 1871 (works number 2139). It is one of four outside cylinder saddle tank engines built for the railway and is typical of many shunting tank engines of the period. It is at present stored at the RENFE Workshops at Valladolid and is intended for the Railway Museum.

Dimensions: CYLINDERS: 330 × 457mm   GRATE AREA: 1.0m²
                  COUPLED WHEELS: 1143mm   BOILER PRESSURE: 10kg/cm²

No 020.0231 is one of ten useful and quite modern-looking 0–4–0 Side Tank locomotives which were built for the Madrid-Zaragoza-Alicante (MZA) in 1885 by Couillet for shunting duties at locomotive depots, factories, docks etc. They have Belpaire boilers, Walschaerts valve gear and originally had copper topped, bell mouthed taper chimneys.

No 020.0231 was MZA No 601 and works number 786. It will be restored for the Railway Museum at present being stored at Aguilas.

No 020.0234 was MZA No 604 built by Couillet works number 789 of 1885 and is a sister-engine to No 020.0231 (above). This locomotive is now owned by the Town Council of Tarrasa and has been restored and put on display in the Avenida del Caudillo in that town.

Dimensions: CYLINDERS: 320 × 460mm
                  COUPLED WHEELS: 992mm
                  GRATE AREA: 0.9m²
                  BOILER PRESSURE: 9kg/cm²

120

No 020.0231 which is preserved [P. R-W

Andaluces No 05 which never carried its RENFE number 020.0241 [P. R-W

No 020.0241 is the RENFE number allocated to but never carried by, Andaluces Railway No 05, an 0–4–0 Side Tank locomotive.

This interesting little engine was built by Tubize (works number 1316) in 1902, one of two for the Company Vecinal de Andalucia which owned a railway connecting Sanlucar de Barrameda with Puerto de Santa-Maria to the north of Cadiz.

The date of the conversion from 2–4–0T to 0–4–0T is not recorded, neither is the date on which it became the property of the Andaluces Railway.

For some years prior to its withdrawal, No 0–5 was shunting at Jerez. It is now preserved and is exhibited in the Station Square at Granada. It remains the property of RENFE.

Dimensions: CYLINDERS: 300 × 400mm
COUPLED WHEELS: 900mm
GRATE AREA: 0.7m^2
BOILER PRESSURE: 12kg/cm^2

No 020.0261 is an outside-cylinder 0–4–0 Side Tank locomotive which was No 31 of the Central of Aragon Railway. It is the first of two locomotives built in 1898 by Couillet (works number 1245), for working between the marshalling yards and the docks at Valencia.

They had Walschaerts valve gear operating slide valves above the cylinders and they were a larger and more powerful version of the MZA engines of the 020.0231–0240 series (qv).

No 020.0261 is at present at Valencia Termiño Depot and is to be preserved in the Railway Museum.

Dimensions: CYLINDERS: 340 × 460mm
COUPLED WHEELS: 1050mm
GRATE AREA: 1.25m^2
BOILER PRESSURE: 12kg/cm^2

No 120.0202 which is a sister engine to No 120.0201   [R. G. Farr

No 120.0201 is an inside cylinder 2–4–0 Side Tank which was built as a 2–4–0 tender engine in 1877 by Sharp Stewart (works number 2708). It was No 23, the first of six (Nos 23–28) for the Tarragona, Barcelona and France Railway which became part of the Madrid-Zaragoza-Alicante (MZA) in 1891.

All six engines were converted to 2–4–0T by MZA in 1901 who numbered them 176–178 respectively. Four survived to be taken into RENFE stock.

Although the reconstructions were carried out in Spain, these engines were very English in appearance and with their high side-tanks and original chimneys must have born a strong resemblance to the "Metropolitan tanks" of the Great Western Railway.

No 120.0201 is stored at Cuenca Locomotive Depot but its future is uncertain.

Dimensions: CYLINDERS: 432 × 610mm
           COUPLED WHEELS: 1712mm
           GRATE AREA: 1.4m²
           BOILER PRESSURE: 8kg/cm²

No 168 was built in 1854 by Sharp Stewart (Atlas Works number 859) as No 4 of the Barcelona Martorell Railway which became part of the Taragona, Barcelona and France Railway. It was a 2–4–0 with outside frames and inside cylinders and motion. A round-topped firebox was surmounted by a safety valve with a bonnet similar to that used by the Great Western Railway of England.

When the Tarragona, Barcelona and France Railway was taken over by the Madrid-Zaragoza-Alicante (MZA) it became No 168 of that railway and its surviving sister engine became No 167. On the occasion of the Barcelona International Exposition of 1929–30, No 168 was converted to a 2–4–0T. It was allocated number 120.2112 on the formation of RENFE in 1941 and, this number implies a 2–4–0 tender engine since tank engines numbers all commence with "0".

This locomotive has been restored and is at present in the *Museum Talleres Generales de Clot* at Barcelona.

Dimensions: CYLINDERS: 381 × 508mm
            COUPLED WHEELS: 1712mm
            GRATE AREA: 1.3m^2
            BOILER PRESSURE: 8kg/cm^2

4–4–0T No 11 BASCONIA   [D. Trevor Rowe

No 11 *BASCONIA* is an outside-cylinder 4–4–0 Side Tank locomotive built
in 1863 by Beyer Peacock (works number 293) for the important 250km
Bilbao-Tudela Railway which became part of the Northern Railway
(*Norte*) under whom No 11 became No 29 *IZARRA*. The locomotive was
sold, in 1927, to S.A. Bascoñia, Echevarri, Bilbao and, until recently, it
was stored at their steel works awaiting possible preservation in the
Railway Museum.
Dimensions: NOT KNOWN

No 030.0201 SAR at work at Vigo Locomotive Works   [P. R-W

No 030.0201 *SAR* is stored in the locomotive depot at Vigo and is likely
to be preserved. It is a little inside-cylinder 0–6–0 Saddle Tank which
was built in 1880 by Hunslet (works number 243) for the West Galicia
Railway (Santiago, Pontevedra-Carril). It carried no number. The
owning company amalgamated with the Medina del Campo, Zamora,
Orense and Vigo Railway which in turn became part of the National
Western Railway (*Oeste*). The *Oeste* gave the engine number 191 and
in 1941 it achieved its present RENFE number.

Dimensions: CYLINDERS: 330 × 400mm
             COUPLED WHEELS: 940mm
             GRATE AREA: 0.7m²
             BOILER PRESSURE: 8kg/cm²

No 030.0202 *JIMENA* is at Utrera depot where it was shed pilot for many years and it is scheduled for preservation. This is an outside-cylinder 0–6–0 tank locomotive with a flat-topped saddle tank. It was built in 1882 by Robert Stephenson (works number 2522) for the contractors building the Algeciras-Bobadilla Railway who, when the line was completed, bought the engine and gave it its number, 20. In 1913 the railway was taken over by the Andaluces Railway and this, in turn, became part of RENFE in 1941 when No 20 became No 030.0202.

Dimensions: CYLINDERS: 355 × 508mm
COUPLED WHEELS: 1079mm
GRATE AREA: 0.7m²
BOILER PRESSURE: 6.3kg/cm²

No 030.0204 TARRACO   [P. R-W

No 030.0204 *TARRACO* is an 0–6–0 Side Tank locomotive built in 1864 by Schneider (works number 743). It is one of five such engines which were the first tank locomotives to be built for the Northern Railway (*Norte*). They all carried names but *TARRACO* was originally *Norte* No 1602 *EL TERA*. For many years it worked the railway staff train between the locomotive depot and the main station at Tarragona. It was painted apple-green, lined out in gold and black and had a burnished copper chimney top. It has been restored and is at present at the *Museum Talleres Generales de Clot* at Barcelona.

Dimensions: CYLINDERS: 350 × 440mm
COUPLED WHEELS: 1000mm
GRATE AREA: 0.8m²
BOILER PRESSURE: 8kg/cm²

No 030.0206 *EL SELMO* and No 030.0207 *EL BURBIA* are 0–6–0 Side Tank locomotives built in 1864 for the Northern Railway (*Norte*) by Schneider (works numbers 745 and 746 respectively). They are sister engines to and are identical with No 030.0204 already described.

These locomotives have been restored and are owned by Señor Lewin Auginalde. They are on display in the garden of his home at Aravaca near Madrid.

PALAU, a sister engine to No 030.0233   [RENFE

No 030.0233 *CALDAS* is an 0–6–0 Side Tank locomotive and was one of the first locomotives to be built in Spain. It is La Maquinista works number 6 of 1888.

It was one of two to be built for the Mollet to Caldas Railway which connected Mollet, on the main line from Barcelona to the north, with Mollet de Montbuy. The company went into liquidation in 1940 and RENFE purchased the two locomotives, Nos 5 and 6 (030.0232 and 0233) together with a third, No 7, built in 1915 and which became 030.0234 in RENFE stock. No 030.0233 is now preserved in the *Museum Talleres Generales de Clot* in Barcelona.

Dimensions: CYLINDERS: 410 × 600mm
COUPLED WHEELS: 1200mm
GRATE AREA: 1.3m²
BOILER PRESSURE: 9kg/cm²

2–6–0ST No 130.0201 PUCHETA   [Brian Garvin

No 130.0201 *PUCHETA* is a 2–6–0 Saddle Tank with outside-cylinders and inside Stephenson link motion. It was built in 1887 by Sharp Stewart (works number 3405) as No 13 for the Triano Railway, a short mineral line extending north-westwards from the environs of Bilbao to San Julian de Musques. This locomotive has the distinction of being the only 2–6–0T ever to run on the Spanish broad gauge. It is at present in store at Logrono and will eventually go to the Railway Museum.

Dimensions: CYLINDERS: 457 × 610mm
               COUPLED WHEELS: 1231mm
               GRATE AREA: 1.5m²
               BOILER PRESSURE: 10kg/cm²

SPAIN 4–6–2 + 2–6–4 Garratt 1674mm

No 464.F.0402 which was identical with the preserved oil-burning Garratt locomotive [P. R-W

No 462.F.0401 is a 4–6–2 + 2–6–4 express passenger Garratt locomotive which was built in 1930 by Euskalduna (works number 191). It is at present stored at Valencia-Alameda Depot for future preservation in the Railway Museum.

Six of these locomotives were built in 1930–31 by Euskalduna, Bilbao for the Central of Aragon Railway on which they were Nos 101–106. They became RENFE Nos 462.0401–0406 in 1941. They were built as hand-fired coal burners but were later all converted to burn oil fuel and so became Nos 462.F.0401–0406. They were distinguished by having large saddle-shaped sand boxes which straddled the leading tanks.

Comparatively few Garratt locomotives were built for express passenger services and these six were designed for duties over the mountainous Central of Aragon line between Valencia and Calatayud. However, in RENFE service, after 1941, they were used almost entirely on the very heavy express trains from France, down the east coast via Barcelona to Valencia, taking over from electric locomotives at Tarragona and working between there and Valencia.

Dimensions: CYLINDERS (4): 484 × 660mm
COUPLED WHEELS: 1750mm
GRATE AREA: 4.9m^2
BOILER PRESSURE: 14kg/cm^2
SUPERHEATED

131

No 9091 the Sentinel Railcar which is to be preserved   [R. G. Farr

No 9091 is a Sentinel Patent Steam Railcar which was built in 1929 by Sentinel Cammel (works number 7604) for the 179.5km-long Zafra-Huelva Railway as their No XF 1001. It was rebuilt in 1933 by Sentinel Construcciones Mécanicas del Llobregat and is at present stored at San Jeronimo Depot, Seville pending preservation.

Details: SIX-CYLINDER SENTINEL ENGINE operating at 500 rpm (maximum) and developing 100 IHP

BOILER PRESSURE: 20kg/cm^2

MECHANICAL TRANSMISSION

MAXIMUM SPEED: 80km/h

Narrow Gauge Locomotive Preservation in Spain

Spain had a very large number of narrow gauge railways owned by private and industrial companies and located in many different parts of the country. To-day, many of these have ceased operating in the face of increasing road competition, a few are still working, having adopted diesel traction, and others are electrified. Many of the remaining narrow gauge lines are now operated by the state under the title *Ferrocarriles de Via Estrecha (FEVE)*.

The most common narrow gauge in Spain is 1000mm but gauges of 1435mm, 1067mm, 914mm, 760mm and 600mm have also been used and some remain.

Spanish narrow gauge steam locomotives were, like their broad gauge sisters, of various designs and widely differing types. Many were of considerable technical interest and it is, therefore, a matter of great regret that only a few are to be preserved. None is included in the prospectus of exhibits for the National Railway Museum. Those that are preserved are on exhibition in public places.

Castilian Secondary Railways No 2 RIOSECO   [R. G. Farr

Castilian Secondary Railways No 2 *RIOSECO* is an outside-cylinder 0–4–0 Side Tank locomotive which was built in 1884 by Sharp Stewart (works number 3231) for the Valladolid to Medina de Rioseco Railway which later became a major part of the Castilian Secondary Railways.

No 2 is preserved in a park on the river bank in Vallodolid and there may be some confusion as to its true identity as it carries its own name and number on one side and that of a sister engine, No 1 *VALLODOLID*, on the other!

Nos 1 and 2 were two of six identical tram engines with the usual iron plate skirting protecting the motion. At some time, side tanks were extended to the length of the boiler, the tank tops being level with the top of the boiler.

Dimensions: NOT KNOWN

Tortosa-La Cava Railway No 1   [D. Trevor Rowe

No 1 of the 27.2km Tortosa-La Cava Railway (FEVE) is an outside-cylinder 4–4–0T built in 1890 by Hunslet (works number 518) and one of three such locomotives which operated the line. They were similar in appearance to some of the 4–4–0T on the narrow gauge railways of Ireland.

No 1 is preserved and is on display in a park near the old terminus of the line in Tortosa.

Dimensions: NOT KNOWN

(The Tortosa-La Cava Railway was operated by Ferrocarriles Económicos S.A. at the time the photograph was taken. It later came into FEVE ownership and has now been closed.)

No 1 *ZUGASTIETA* of the 30.4km Amorebieta, Guernica and Bermeo (FEVE) Railway was built in 1888 by Sharp Stewart (works number 3435). It is an outside-cylinder 0–6–0T and is preserved and on display at Guernica.
Dimensions: NOT KNOWN

No 6 of the 139.2km Vasco-Navarro Railway in the north of Spain, is an outside-cylinder 0–6–0T built in 1892 by St. Leonard (works number 920). It has been preserved by the *Asociacion de Amigos del Ferrocarril de Bilbao* and is on display at the Basurto Station at Bilbao. It occasionally works special trains.
Dimensions: NOT KNOWN

No 103 *ORCANERA* is an 0–6–0 Side Tank locomotive built in 1881 by Hanomag (works number 1459) as No 4 of the Bilbao to Durango Railway. It later came into the ownership of the important mineral railway, owned by the *Compania Minera de Sierra Menera*, which gave the engine its present number and name. No 103 is now preserved at the Steel Works of the Altos Hornes Company of Vizcaya at Sagunto.
Dimensions: NOT KNOWN

No 33 is an outside-cylinder 0–6–0 Side Tank locomotive built in 1902 for the *Compania General de Ferrocarriles Catalanes SA (CGFC)* by La Maquinista (works number 35). It has been painted green and put on display on a plinth at Martorell Empalme.
Dimensions: NOT KNOWN

No 104 *AURRERA* is an outside-cylinder 2–6–0T which was built in 1894 by Nasmyth Wilson (works number 456) for the Vascongados Railway Company which operates 257 route kilometres of (now) electrified railway. No 104 was restored to its original condition and stored at Durango for preservation but is still occasionally used for shunting duties.

Dimensions: NOT KNOWN

No 1 of the 40.6km Onda al Grao de Castellon (FEVE) Railway is an outside-cylinder 0–6–0T built in 1888 by Krauss (works number 1984). This little engine is painted green and is on display opposite to the RENFE station at Castellon north of Sagunto on the East Coast.

Dimensions: NOT KNOWN

Swedish State Railways

Statens Järnväger, SJ, began railway construction in Sweden in 1855. The first railways in Sweden were privately-built narrow gauge lines, standard gauge being introduced in 1856. Private railways continued to be built in considerable profusion but, from 1879, the State Railways began absorbing many of them and the process continued until recent years. At the present time SJ owns and operates about 90 per cent of the standard gauge lines in the country. It also operates a considerable kilometrage of narrow gauge railways though many of these, as well as most of the remaining privately-owned narrow gauge railways, have been closed to traffic in the last twenty years.

Swedish State Railways Locomotives

In the early years of Swedish railways, locomotives were supplied from Britain, mainly from Beyer, Peacock and Sharp, Stewart, and from Germany, mainly from Borsig. Later, most locomotives in Sweden were built by domestic builders such as Nydquist and Holm, Motala and Munktells. The first locomotive to be built in Sweden was an 0–4–0 for the 891mm (three Swedish feet) gauge. It was named *FÖRSTLINGEN* and was built by Munktells in 1853. It was later converted to 1435mm gauge.

As with other Scandinavian locomotives, those in Sweden were considerably limited by the fact that only a light axle load was permissible on many routes. As a result, there were comparatively few powerful steam locomotives in Sweden though many interesting and highly individual designs were evolved.

The SJ had a fairly simple method of locomotive classification and this was adopted also by most private railways. In the beginning every class was designated by a capital letter, A, B, C and so on. When locomotives required reboilering a small letter was added to both the original and the reboilered engines: thus locomotives in their original state became Aa, Ba, Ca and so on, while those with new boilers were Ab, Bb, Cb, etc. Later, new and improved boilers, often with superheaters, were fitted and these were signified by numbers in the classification: Ab1, Ab2, Bb1 and so on. To complicate matters, however, the small letter also came to be used to denote rebuilding in other ways than reboilering, for example Class Ca was a reboilered 2–4–0 of Class C but Classes Cb and Cc were locomotives of Class C which were rebuilt as 4–4–0

Steam Locomotive Preservation in Sweden

Swedish Railways have been very "Preservation-minded" for much longer than have most other European railways. As early as 1890, interesting relics were being preserved for a future railway museum, and the first such museum was opened in May 1915 at Klarabergsgaten, 70 in Stockholm. The museum moved to larger premises at Vasagatan, 3 in 1932 and in 1941 the locomotive shed at Tomteboda, outside Stockholm was made available to house a very fine and representative collection of locomotives and rolling stock of both standard and narrow gauge.

While the "full size" relics remained at Tomteboda for nearly 30 years, the museum at Vasagatan was forced to close in 1946 and most of the models and relics have been in store until 1970.

Now, Sweden has, at last, obtained at Gävle, museum premises which are large enough, and very suitable, for the display of all the smaller items as well as for all the locomotives and rolling stock from the Tomteboda Museum which is now closed.

While the principal museum is at Gävle, other museums such as those at Trelleborg and at Kristianstad have acquired withdrawn locomotives and rolling stock while others are preserved in the open at various places. It is understood that a representative collection of the TGOJ is to be preserved in a museum at Eskilstuna.

It is possible that some locomotives will be preserved in working order and that they will be used on "Museum Railways" operated by enthusiasts. Perhaps the most viable of these 1435mm-gauge projects is Foreningen Skanska Jarnvag, Brosarp which hopes to operate over the Kristianstad-Ahus line.

Finally, mention must be made of those steam locomotives which are maintained in working order as a strategic motive power reserve. The location and number of these locomotives is confidential military information.

SJ 2–2–2 No 75 GÖTA   [R. G. Farr

SJ No 75 *GÖTA* original Class A, later Aa, is an outside-cylinder 2–2–2 built in 1866 by Beyer, Peacock (works number 627). It was restored in 1906 and exhibited in the Railway Museum first at Tomteboda and now at Gävle.

Twenty-two Class A "simples" were built for SJ by Beyer, Peacock (18) and Nydquist (4) and they had slide valves between the cylinders actuated by Allan link motion. They had domed round-top boilers and copper-topped chimneys. Most, but not all, were rebuilt with Belpaire boilers and with side-sheets to the original open cabs. Originally they had one cross-head feed pump and one injector. Those engines never rebuilt were Class Aa and the rebuilds became Ab 1 or Ab 2 according to the boiler heating surface. All, during their lives, had Swedish type spark arresters.

These 2–2–2s were almost identical with ten engines built for the Netherlands State Railways at the same time by Beyer, Peacock.

Dimensions: CYLINDERS: 381 × 508mm
DRIVING WHEELS: 1880mm
GRATE AREA: 1.3m²
BOILER PRESSURE: 7kg/cm²

SJ 2–4–0 No 3 PRINS AUGUST

[R. G. Farr

SJ No 3 *PRINS AUGUST* Class Ba 1 (original Class B) is a 2–4–0 locomotive with outside cylinders and inside Allan link motion built for SJ in 1856 by Beyer, Peacock (works number 33) and now preserved in the Railway Museum at Gävle.   It has been restored to its original condition with domeless round-top boiler, copper-topped chimney and with a crosshead, driven feed water pump on the Left hand side and a steam driven-reciprocating feed pump with flywheel, on the Right hand side.

Forty-six Class B mixed traffic engines were supplied between 1856 and 1873 and they were the first engines to be built for SJ. Beyer Peacock, Nyköping, Motala and Nydquist supplied them and they were excellent machines, speedy and economical.   They varied in detail, mainly in boiler pressures and heating surfaces and there were four sub-divisions of the class. During their lives they were renumbered (No 3 became 43) and reboilered with Belpaire boilers.   They also had chimneys with Swedish-type spark arresters and the feed-water pumps were replaced by injectors. Also, the weather boards gave way to quite commodious cabs but they retained the four-wheel tenders.   The last engines of the class were withdrawn in 1909.

Dimensions: CYLINDERS: 394 × 508mm
              COUPLED WHEELS: 1680mm
              GRATE AREA: 1.4m²
              BOILER PRESSURE: as built: 7kg/cm²
                          as reboilered: 10kg/cm²

SJ No 347 Class Da 2 is a mixed traffic outside-cylinder 2–4–0 with inside Allan link motion built for SJ in 1886 by Motala (works number 82). It is preserved in the Railway Museum at Gävle.

Class D consisted of 50 locomotives built in batches between 1874 and 1887 by Borsig, Nydquist and Motala to the designs of the first Chief Mechanical Engineer of SJ, Frederick A. Almgren. The first 35 were Class Da 1 which had 154 fire tubes against 140 of the later engines of Class Da 2. They had a Salter safety valve on the dome and a spring-loaded valve with a pillar-type cover on top of the Belpaire firebox. Later, Swedish spark arresters were fitted and some engines were wood burners. The class became extinct in 1927; No 347 was preserved on being withdrawn in 1921.

Dimensions: CYLINDERS: 394 × 508mm   GRATE AREA: 1.7m²
           COUPLED WHEELS: 1562mm   BOILER PRESSURE: 10kg/cm²

SJ 2–4–0 No 198 BREDA   [Brian Garvin

SJ No 198 *BREDA* Class Ca is an outside-cylinder 2–4–0 with inside Allan link motion which was built in 1875 by Borsig (works number 3427). It has been restored and is now preserved in the Railway Museum at Gävle.

Twenty-four locomotives of Class Ca were built in batches between 1875 and 1883 by Borsig, Nydquist and Motala. They were the standard express locomotives of the period and were designed by F. A. Almgren who had them embellished with green paint and polished brass. Most of these locomotives were later given larger, six-wheel tenders and they were all coal burners.

Locomotives of Class Ca were very similar to those of Class Da (qv) but they had larger diameter coupled wheels.

Dimensions: CYLINDERS: 394 × 508mm   GRATE AREA: 1.7m²
           COUPLED WHEELS: 1626mm   BOILER PRESSURE: 10kg/cm²

143

TGOJ 0–4–2 No 8

[Brian Garvin

Trafik AB Grangesberg Oxelösunds Railway (TGOJ) No 8 is an inside-cylinder 0–4–2 locomotive with four-wheeled tender, very English in appearance. It was built in 1876 by Sharp, Stewart (works number 2597) for the Oxelösund Flen Västmanlands Railway (OFWJ). It went to TGOJ in 1931 and was withdrawn and presented to the Railway Museum in 1956. It is now exhibited at Gävle.

Dimensions: CYLINDERS: 381 × 559mm
COUPLED WHEELS: 1555mm
GRATE AREA: 1.0m^2
BOILER PRESSURE: 9atm

SJ 4–4–0 No 404 [Railway Museum SJ

SJ No 404 Class Cc is an outside-cylinder 4–4–0 locomotive designed by Frederick A. Almgren and built in 1892 by Nydquist (works number 323). It is preserved in the Railway Museum at Gävle.

The previous class of 4–4–0 locomotives of Class Cb had proved to be too small and underboilered for the fast passenger train duties they were called upon to perform. The bogie coach was introduced into Sweden in 1891 and with the consequent increase in the weights of trains, a new and more powerful machine was essential. Class Cc appeared in 1892 and, during the next eleven years, 79 were built. They had bogies with bar frames and the bogie pin was located behind the second axle. The round-top boilers were much bigger than the Belpaire boilers of Class Cb and the frames and running plates were stronger.

One engine of Class Cc was built as a two-cylinder Gölsdorf compound, another had a Brotan boiler. During their lives, several burned wood and one was fitted for burning powdered peat on the Ekelund system. The steam chests were above the outside cylinders and the balanced slide valves were actuated by inside Allan link motion through rocking shafts. The original ten boilers had a pressure of 10kg/cm² and this was raised to 11kg/cm² in new boilers which were fitted to all the engines between 1905 and 1910. Forty-eight were superheated to become Class Cd and when new boilers were fitted the pressure was again raised to 12kg/cm².

The previous Class Cb were all rebuilt with larger boilers to Class Cc in 1903–05.

Class Cc was never up to the work it was required to do and most trains had to be double-headed if they were to keep time. None the less, some of them were still in service as late as 1956.

Dimensions: CYLINDERS: 420 × 560mm
COUPLED WHEELS: 1880mm
GRATE AREA: 1.86m²
BOILER PRESSURE: 11kg/cm²

SJ 4-4-0 No 1774   [Ulf Diehl

SJ No 1774 Class C-7 is an inside-cylinder 4-4-0 with Stephenson link motion and with a four-wheeled tender which was built in 1904 by Nydquist (works number 740). It was originally No 51, Class C of the Bergslagernas Railway (BJ) and, after being superheated in 1915, became their Class C-3. It was sold to the Nassjö Oskarsham Railway in 1941 becoming their No. 37. SJ assumed ownership of this locomotive in 1946. No 1774 is now on display at Hultsfred Hembygdsparken.

SJ No 1814 Class C-7 is a sister to No 1774 and was built in 1905 by Nydquist (works number 775). It went to SJ direct from BJ in 1947. It has the distinction of having been the first superheated locomotive in Sweden. It is at present in store at Älmhult and its future is doubtful.

Dimensions: CYLINDERS: 440 × 610mm
           COUPLED WHEELS: 1722mm
           GRATE AREA: 1.7m^2
           BOILER PRESSURE: 10kg/cm^2
           SUPERHEATED

SJ 4–4–2 No 1024, identical with No 1001   [Drawing by the late H. M. le Fleming

SJ No 1001 Class A is an inside-cylinder 4–4–2 express locomotive built in 1907 by Motala (works number 378). It has been sectioned and is now exhibited in the Railway Museum at Gävle.

Twenty-five locomotives of Class A were built between 1906 and 1909 by Motala and by Nydquist. They had superheated, round-top fireboxes and the sandbox and dome were under a single cover. Piston valves above the cylinders were driven by inside Walschaerts valve gear. In order to provide clearance of the inside cylinders, the bogies had outside frames and axleboxes. The large and commodious cabs were wedge-shaped.

These locomotives were very prone to slip when hauling heavy trains and four were rebuilt as 4–6–0.

Dimensions: CYLINDERS: 500 × 600mm
         COUPLED WHEELS: 1880mm
         GRATE AREA: 2.6m^2
         BOILER PRESSURE: 12kg/cm^2
         SUPERHEATED

SJ 0–6–0 No 93   [Brian Garvin

SJ No 93 *JERNSIDA* Class Gc (originally Class G) is an inside-cylinder 0–6–0 built in 1867 by Beyer, Peacock (works number 809). It has been restored and is now exhibited in the Railway Museum at Gävle.

Fifty-seven Class Ga locomotives were built between 1866 and 1874. They were supplied in batches by Beyer, Peacock and by Nydquist and were a larger and more powerful design than the previous Class F locomotives which were unable to handle satisfactorily the increasing heavy freight traffic. They had Stephenson link motion with slide valves between the cylinders. The boilers had polished brass dome covers and the brass safety valve covers were identical with those on the Midland Railway of England. The engines were reboilered to Class Gb and later again had new boilers and an alteration in the springing, becoming thus, Class Gc. Some of the class were not withdrawn until 1921.

Dimensions: CYLINDERS: 406 × 610mm
          COUPLED WHEELS: 864mm
          GRATE AREA: 1.4m²
          BOILER PRESSURE: 10kg/cm² (originally 8.5kg/cm²)

Bergslagernas Railway (BJ), inside-cylinder 0–6–0 No 27 Class K was built in 1880 by Beyer, Peacock (works number 1933) and was withdrawn

BJ 0–6–0 No 27   [Brian Garvin

and presented to the Railway Museum in 1956. It has been completely
restored and is now at Gävle.

This locomotive is a typical Beyer Peacock standard freight locomotive
of the period. It has a four-wheeled tender and the valve gear is inside
Stephenson link motion.

BJ 0–6–0 No 1551 Class KA 3   [Brian Garvin

SJ 0–6–0 No 1551 Class KA 3 is identical with BJ No 27. It was, however,
built in 1901 by Nydquist (works number 591) for the Borås Alvesta

149

Railway (BAJ) as their No 3 (later 53) of Class K. It went to SJ in 1940 and was to be purchased by the town of Borås for display in their Nybroparken. At present, however, its future is uncertain.

Dimensions: CYLINDERS: 432 × 610mm
COUPLED WHEELS: 1273mm
GRATE AREA: 1.4m²
BOILER PRESSURE: 9kg/cm²

SJ No 390 Class Kd 1 is an outside-cylinder 0–6–0 locomotive with Allan link motion and balanced slide valves inside the frames. It was built in 1890 by Nydquist (works number 300) and has been restored and placed in the Railway Museum at Gävle.

SJ No 692 Class Kd 2 is of the same type and dimensions as Class Kd 1 above, apart from a small increase in boiler heating surface and a corresponding increase in the weight of the engine in working order. Locomotives of Class Kd 2 also had wider and more commodious cabs.

No 692 was built in 1901 by Falun (works number 1) and it is preserved in the Linköping Museum.

The standard outside-cylinder 0–6–0 freight engines of Class K were introduced in 1875 and the class included a number of sub-classes which generally were improvements, the one over the other. Class Kd were larger and more powerful engines than the preceding Class Kc 5 and 139 were built by various Swedish locomotive builders between 1890 and 1902. This was, numerically, the largest class of locomotives in Sweden. They were excellent machines though heavy on coal and so, many were scrapped in the 1920s. Others were, however, rebuilt with superheaters and, where necessary, new boilers, and these became Class Ka. They had wire mesh spark arresters over the chimney tops in place of the old Swedish type at the base of the chimney. A few of the class were wood-burners and, during World War I, a number was converted to 0–6–2 Side Tank locomotives and burned powdered peat. These were Class Kf, while the classification Kf 2 was given to four superheated coal-burning tank-engine conversions. In 1943 Class Ka became known as Class K and Kf 2 as Class K 2.

Dimensions of Class Kd: CYLINDERS: 450 × 560mm
COUPLED WHEELS: 1372mm
GRATE AREA: 1.65m²
BOILER PRESSURE: 10kg/cm²

SJ No 1668 restored as OSJ No 15   [L. O. Karlsson

Restored to its original condition and exhibited at the Kristianstad Museum is inside-cylinder 2–6–0 No 15 Class G of the Östra Skänes Railway (OSJ). It was built in 1900 by Nydquist (works number 564) and was sold in 1936 to the Kristianstad Hässelholm Railway and became their No 35. In 1944 it went to SJ and was their No 1668 Class L 21.

This locomotive demonstrates in its design the natural evolution of the 0–6–0 into the 2–6–0 when higher speeds and a mixed traffic function were required. The first 2–6–0s in Sweden were all built by domestic firms and they had, with one exception, inside cylinders and valve gear. They usually had larger driving wheels than had the 0–6–0s from which they were evolved. In many instances the radial wheels formed a type of Krauss truck with the leading coupled wheels.

Dimensions: CYLINDERS: 410 × 610mm
             COUPLED WHEELS: 1530mm
             GRATE AREA: 1.37m^2
             BOILER PRESSURE: 11kg/cm^2

SJ 2–6–0 No 1655

[Brian Garvin

SJ No 1655 Class L–11 is a superheated, inside-cylinder 2–6–0 locomotive which was built in 1908 by Motala (works number 421) as No 15 of the Kristianstad-Hässelholm Railway (CHJ). It is preserved in the Railway Museum at Kristianstad.

This locomotive was one of four built for the Kristianstad-Hässelholm Railway, the first two (CHJ Nos 14 and 15) in 1908 and the second two (CHJ Nos 16 and 17) in 1911. They were taken over by SJ in 1944.

The leading coupled wheels form a Krauss truck with the radial wheels and the maximum axle-load is 11 tonnes. The piston valves are above the inside cylinders and steam distribution is by means of inside Walschaerts valve gear.

Dimensions: CYLINDERS: 470 × 610mm
COUPLED WHEELS: 1400mm
GRATE AREA: 1.64m²
BOILER PRESSURE: 11kg/cm²
SUPERHEATED

SJ No 1714 Class L 23   [L. O. Karlsson

SJ inside-cylinder 2–6–0 No 1714 Class L 23 with inside Allan link motion, was built in 1899 by Motala (works number 200). It was originally No 40 of the Stockholm Västerås, Bergslags Railway (SWB) and was first classified G and later F. It was fitted with a superheater in 1928 and became SWB Class F 3a.

SWB was absorbed by SJ and No 40 became SJ No 1714 in 1945. This locomotive has now been withdrawn and is at present in store at Västerås awaiting preservation, probably at the Railway Museum at Gävle.

Dimensions: CYLINDERS: 432 × 610mm
             COUPLED WHEELS: 1550mm
             GRATE AREA: 1.7m²
             BOILER PRESSURE: 11kg/cm²

153

SJ 4–6–0 No 864 Class Tb with peat bunker on tender [Railway Museum SJ

SJ No 864 Class Tb was built in 1906 by Nydquist (works number 798) and is preserved and exhibited in the Railway Museum at Gävle.

No 864 is a two-cylinder compound 4–6–0, one of 36 built between 1905 and 1908 for fast freight and heavy passenger train duties.

The design originated with Class Ta which was introduced in 1899 and of which the first ten were built by the Richmond Locomotive Works in the USA, largely to American standards of the period.

Class Tb were similar but had altered boiler dimensions and a larger grate area than Class Ta. They had bar frames but the bogies had plate frames. The cylinders were outside, the high pressure being on the Left hand and the low pressure on the Right hand side of the engine. Balanced slide valves on top of the cylinders were operated by inside Stephenson link motion through rocking shafts. Some of the engines, temporarily, had Clench steam driers but neither Class Ta nor Tb were ever superheated. They had wire-mesh spark arresters in the chimneys.

Seven engines of Class Ta and 10 of Class Tb were sold to the Finnish State Railways in 1942, the alteration to the Finnish 1524mm gauge being achieved by altering the wheel centres by heating and then drop forging them to an altered form.

No 864 is preserved as a peat-burner, the powdered peat being carried in a large bunker on the tender. It also has both air and vacuum brakes.

Dimensions: CYLINDERS: HIGH PRESSURE: 508 × 610mm
LOW PRESSURE: 788 × 610mm
COUPLED WHEELS: 1580mm
GRATE AREA: 2.4m^2
BOILER PRESSURE: 14kg/cm^2

SJ 4–6–0 No 1314 Class B which is identical with the preserved locomotive [P. R-W

SJ No 1026 Class B is an outside-cylinder superheated 4–6–0 built in 1909 by Motala (works number 431). It is in reserve but is scheduled for probable preservation in the Railway Museum at Gävle.

The 98 locomotives of Class B and of which No 1026 was the first, were built for SJ between 1909 and 1919 and they formed numerically the largest class of passenger engines in Sweden. A further three were built in 1943–44 for the Stockholm-Västerås-Bergslags Railway which was absorbed by SJ in 1945 and thus these three engines also came into SJ stock.

These are fine modern locomotives with piston valves above the cylinders operated by Walschaerts valve gear. They have bar frames but the bogie frames are of plate and are outside the wheels. The smokebox has a conical front and the wire-mesh spark arrester is inside the chimney.

A large bogie tender is fitted to most of the engines and adds to their excellent and well-balanced appearance.

Dimensions: CYLINDERS: 590 × 620mm
COUPLED WHEELS: 1750mm
GRATE AREA: 2.6m^2
BOILER PRESSURE: 12kg/cm^2
SUPERHEATED

SJ No 4–6–2 No 1200 Class F

[Brian Garvin

SJ No 1200 Class F is a four-cylinder compound 4–6–2 built in 1914 by Nydquist (works number 1020). It is preserved in working order and is at present at the SJ depot at Östersund.

The 11 locomotives of Class F, of which No 1200 was the prototype, were the first of the Pacific type in Scandinavia. They were all built by Nydquist between 1914 and 1916 to work on the increasingly heavy main line express services which were getting beyond the capabilities of the Class B 4–6–0s. They became at once very popular with their drivers and were proved to be easily masters of their work.

They were four-cylinder Vauclain balanced compounds with the high pressure cylinders inside the frames and the low pressure outside. Each pair of high pressure and low pressure cylinders had a common piston valve operated by outside Walschaerts valve gear. Cylinder by-pass valves were fitted and the engines could work as two-cylinder simples using either the two high pressure or the two low pressure cylinders. The four cylinders were in line, inclined and all drove the second coupled axle.

The engines had plate frames, the bogie frames being outside the wheels. The trailing axles were in Cartazzi axle-boxes. The cabs had wooden sides and wedge shaped fronts.

The boilers were large and had round-top fireboxes with wide grates. The sand and steam domes were in the same cover. Schmidt superheaters were fitted.

As a result of the electrification of the Swedish main lines, the Class F locomotives became redundant and, in 1937, they were sold at a very low price to the Danish State Railways who, after reconditioning and converting them to Right-hand drive, put them into service as their Class E on the main lines in Jutland and Zealand. No 1200 was DSB No 964 and it returned to Sweden for preservation in exchange for SJ No 975, an 0–10–0 of Class R which was of equivalent weight in scrap metal. (The Danes are not allowed by law to export scrap metal.)

Between 1942 and 1950, Frichs built 25 more of these engines for DSB. These had minor alterations in that they had hopper ash pans, steel cabs and an extra dome housing a steam drier. Fifteen of the DSB engines had Lemaître double blast pipes and chimneys.

Dimensions: CYLINDERS: HIGH PRESSURE: 420×660mm
                               LOW PRESSURE: 630×660mm
             COUPLED WHEELS: 1880mm
             GRATE AREA: 3.6m^2
             BOILER PRESSURE: 13kg/cm^2
             SUPERHEATED

SJ 0–8–0 No 1460 Class E was similar to No 900   [P. R-W

SJ No 900 is a superheated inside-cylinder 0–8–0 freight engine built in 1907 by Nydquist (works number 829). It is in reserve but is scheduled for probable preservation in the Railway Museum at Gävle.

No 900 was the first of 130 locomotives of Class E which were supplied in batches by various Swedish builders between 1907 and 1920. They could work over most of the SJ lines, having a maximum axle-load of only 12.5 tonnes and a short wheelbase. Many of the class were rebuilt as 2–8–0.

Dimensions: CYLINDERS: 500 × 640mm
             COUPLED WHEELS: 1388mm
             GRATE AREA: 2.08m^2
             BOILER PRESSURE: 12kg/cm^2
             SUPERHEATED

SJ 2–8–0 No 779 Class Ma   [Railway Museum SJ

SJ No 779 Class Ma is a Mellin two-cylinder compound 2–8–0 built in 1904 by Nydquist (works number 730). It is preserved and exhibited in the Railway Museum at Gävle.

Two classes of 2–8–0 came into service in 1901 (Class Mb) and 1902 (Class Ma). Class Mb was the lighter by about 10 tonnes but the difference between the classes was only in the size of the boiler and the working pressure. They had Schmidt superheaters.

Both classes were designed for working heavy iron-ore trains on the Kiruna-Narvik line and Class Ma could haul 1,000-tonne trains on the level and could take 1,100 tonnes up a 1 in 90 (11 $^0/_{00}$) gradient with banking assistance. The locomotives had plate frames and the leading wheels formed a Krauss truck with the first pair of coupled wheels.

There were 21 engines of Class Ma and they were not very successful. A trial was made with one engine rebuilt with two high pressure cylinders but the boiler could not supply sufficient steam. The best results were obtained from two which were rebuilt with larger compound cylinders and piston valves replacing the former balanced slide valves. All the Class Ma had Helmholz valve gear, a modification of Walschaerts with a straight expansion link. The high pressure cylinder was on the Left hand and the low pressure on the Right hand side of the engine.

Dimensions: CYLINDERS: HIGH PRESSURE: 530 × 640mm
                    LOW PRESSURE: 810 × 640mm
          COUPLED WHEELS: 1296mm
          GRATE AREA: 2.9m^2
          BOILER PRESSURE: 14kg/cm^2

SOEJ 2–4–0T No 1   [L. O. Karlsson]

No 1 of the Sölvesborg Olofström Elmhults Railway (SOEJ) is a small outside cylinder 2–4–0 Side Tank locomotive built in 1890 by Munktells (works number 25) for the Nassjö Oskarsham Railway (NOJ) as their No 12 *SJÖGLE*. It was sold to SOEJ in 1923 and in 1943 went to Motala Verkstads. The locomotive was withdrawn in 1949 and, ten years later, it was restored and placed on display on the station platform in Älmhult.

Dimensions: CYLINDERS: 320 × 450mm
                 COUPLED WHEELS: 1200mm
                 GRATE AREA: 0.8m²
                 BOILER PRESSURE: 10kg/cm²

UWHJ 2-4-0T TROLLHÄTTAN   [Railway Museum SJ

Uddevalla-Wenersborg-Herrljunga Railway (UWHJ) No 1 *TROLL-HÄTTAN* is an outside-cylinder 2–4–0 Side Tank locomotive with inside Stephenson link motion. It was built for the UWHJ in 1865 by the famous Trollhättan firm of Nydquist and Holm Actiebolag (later abbreviated to NOHAB) and was their works number 1. It is now preserved in the Railway Museum at Gävle.

TRÖLLHATTAN was copied from a similar locomotive which had been built for the Boräs-Herrljunga Railway by Slaughter, Grunning of Bristol in 1863, and it was in regular service until 1899 when the gauge of the UWHJ was changed to 1435mm.

Dimensions: CYLINDERS: 280 × 407mm
          COUPLED WHEELS: 990mm
          GRATE AREA: 0.56m²
          BOILER PRESSURE: 10kg/cm²

SJ 0–4–2T No 22 THOR   [Brian Garvin

SJ No 22 *THOR* Class Qä is an inside-cylinder 0–4–2 Saddle Tank loco-motive with a domeless boiler, built in 1861 by Beyer, Peacock (works number 239). It is restored to its original condition apart from retaining the cab which was a later addition. *THOR* is exhibited at the Railway Museum at Gävle.

Six of these 0–4–2ST were delivered by Beyer, Peacock to the State Railways between 1858 and 1879 and they were stationed at the Central Depot at Stockholm for use on construction trains. The first two were SJ Nos 21 and 22, the last four were Nos 3, 4, 5, 6 of the Central Depot. In 1895, the six engines became SJ Nos 505–510 respectively and were Class A. In 1900 they were classified Qä.

The slide valves were between the cylinders and were operated by inside Stephenson link motion.

Dimensions: CYLINDERS: 356 × 508mm
COUPLED WHEELS: 1220mm
GRATE AREA: 0.9m²
BOILER PRESSURE: 8.5kg/cm² (10kg/cm² with later boiler)

HHyJ 4–4–0T No 1, as LKN No 5 [T. Romsloe

No 5 is a 4–4–0 Well Tank locomotive with outside cylinders and Allan link motion operating slide valves above the cylinders.

It was built in 1882 by Nydquist (works number 160) for the Höör-Hörby Railway (HHyJ) and was No 1 *BIFROST* on that railway. In 1900 it was sold to the Swedish iron-ore company Luossavaara-Kirunavaara AB of Narvik, Norway, and became their No 5. It retains its Swedish spark arrester above the smokebox.

This locomotive was withdrawn in 1964 and is now in Narvik NSB depot having been restored and purchased privately for preservation.

Dimensions: CYLINDERS: 310 × 445mm
      COUPLED WHEELS: 868mm
      GRATE AREA: 1.1m^2
      BOILER PRESSURE: 10kg/cm^2

TGOJ No 55 Class S 3 which was identical with the preserved locomotive   [L. O. Karlsson

No 15 is a superheated 2–4–4 Side Tank locomotive with outside cylinders, piston valves and Walschaerts valve gear. It was built in 1923 by Motala (works number 703) for the Landskrona Lund Trälleborg Railway (LLTJ) and in 1938 it came into the ownership of Trafik AB Grängesberg Oxelösunds Railway (TGOJ) as their No 91 of Class S3. No 15 is now preserved in the museum at Trelleborg.

When No 15 went to the TGOJ it joined a stud of eight identical locomotives, six (Nos 51–56) of which had been taken over from the Oxelösund, Flen, Västermanlands Railway (OFWJ) in 1931 and two (Nos 57–58) which had been built for TGOJ in 1936. The design is that of a very handsome and well-balanced locomotive of essentially modern appearance. The steam dome is located ahead of the sand dome but in the same casing.

Dimensions: CYLINDERS: 460 × 600mm
COUPLED WHEELS: 1712mm
GRATE AREA: 1.9m^2
BOILER PRESSURE: 11atm
SUPERHEATED

SWEDEN 0–6–0T 1435mm

OFWJ No 1 Class U-2 when in store during 1958 [L. O. Karlsson

No 1 Class U–2 of the Oxelösund, Flen, Västermanlands Railway (OFWJ) is an 0–6–0 Saddle Tank locomotive with a domeless boiler and inside cylinders. It was built in 1874 by Sharp, Stewart (works number 2428) and came into the ownership of Trafik AB Grängesberg-Oxelösunds Railway (TGOJ) in 1924. In 1930 it was placed in the TGOJ Museum at Eskilstuna.

Dimensions: CYLINDERS: 381 × 508mm
COUPLED WHEELS: 1372mm
GRATE AREA: 0.93mm
BOILER PRESSURE: 10kg/cm²

No 1 *KARLSKOGA* of the Nora Karlskoga Railway (NKJ) is an outside-cylinder 0–6–0 Saddle Tank locomotive built in 1873 by Fox Walker (works number 154) for the Skane Smalands Jarnvag as their No 4. It went to NKJ in 1906.

NKJ 0–6–0ST No 1 KARLSKOGA　　　　　　　　　　　　　　　　[L. O. Karlsson

This locomotive has been restored and is on display outside the railway station at Karlskoga.
Dimensions: NOT KNOWN

MaSJ 0–6–0ST No 3 TYR　　　　　　　　　　　　　　　　　　[L. O. Karlsson

No 3 TYR of the Marma Sandarne Railway (MaSJ) is an inside-cylinder 0–6–0 Saddle Tank locomotive which was built in 1908 by Nydquist (works number 906). The safety valves are mounted on the dome and coal is carried in a bunker at the back of the cab.

This locomotive is now on display in the open at the Stadsparken at Nässjö.
Dimensions: NOT KNOWN

SWEDEN 0–6–0T 1101mm

Frycksta Railway 0–6–0WT FRYCKSTAD [Railway Museum SJ

FRYCKSTAD is an 0–6–0 Well Tank locomotive which was built in 1855 by Munktells and it is reputedly their works number 2 and the second locomotive to have been built in Sweden (the first was an 0–4–0 named *FÖRSTLINGEN* in 1847). *FRYCKSTAD* is now preserved in the Railway Museum at Gävle.

The first private railway in Sweden was the 1101mm-gauge Fryksta Klara Älv Railway (FKAJ) which was built in 1849 to connect the landing place on Lake Fryken with the River Klarelfven. It was operated by horses until this form of motive power was replaced by *FRYCKSTAD*. In 1872 the Frycksta Railway was replaced by a 1435mm-gauge line and the locomotive was sent to work on the fortifications of the naval base at Karlskrona. In 1880 it went to the fortress of Karlsborg but was never used there and it was presented to the Stockholm Railway Museum in 1906.

FRYCKSTAD has sandwich frames, inclined outside cylinders and inside Stephenson link motion.

Dimensions: CYLINDERS: 230 × 395mm
COUPLED WHEELS: 814mm
GRATE AREA: 0.55m²
BOILER PRESSURE: 7kg/cm²

MlSlJ No 2 MALMKÖPING in store before going to Trelleborg Museum [L. O. Karlsson

KNJ No 1 which was a sister engine to the preserved No 2 BJURFORS [L. O. Karlsson

SWEDEN 2–6–0T 1435mm

No 2 *MALMKÖPING* is a 2–6–0 Side Tank locomotive with outside
cylinders and Walschaerts valve gear which was built in 1906 by Nydquist
(works number 810) for the Mellersta Södermanland Railway (MlSlJ) and
it was one of two identical engines supplied at that time. It later became SJ
No 1508 Class MS and in 1936 was sold again, this time to become No 2
of the Bjärred, Lund, Harlösa Railway (BLHJ).

In 1940, it was sold once again, this time to the firm of Svenska Socker
AB Kavlange and Hököpinge. It is frequently reported as being named
Hököpinge but in fact has never carried that name. This locomotive has
been, since 1963, in the museum at Trelleborg.

Dimensions: CYLINDERS: 350 × 510mm
COUPLED WHEELS: 1400mm
GRATE AREA: not known
BOILER PRESSURE: 10kg/cm^2

No 2 *BJURFORS* is an outside-clinder 2–6–0 Side Tank locomotive built in
1891 by Nydquist (works number 327) for the Krylbro Norberg Railway
(KNJ). It was later sold to Avesta Jernverk where it is presently
preserved.

No further details are available.

SJ 0–8–0T No 1130 Class N was of the same class as No 576 [P. R-W

SJ No 576 Class N is an outside-cylinder 0–8–0 Side Tank locomotive built in 1900 by Motala (works number 233). It is still at work at Borås but it is likely to be scheduled for preservation in the Railway Museum at Gävle.

Twenty of these heavy and powerful shunting engines were built in 1900–01. They were the first Swedish locomotives to have totally enclosed cabs. Each had a Swedish type spark arrester, safety valves on top of the large steam dome, and a separate sand dome between the steam dome and the cab. Balanced slide valves were above the cylinders and were operated by Helmholz valve gear. Maximum axle-load was 14.4 tonnes.

During the period 1912–20 a further 44 of the class were built and most of these had the sandbox and dome in a single cover and the safety valves were over the firebox. Later, about two-thirds of the engines in the class were superheated but retained their balanced slide valves.

Dimensions: CYLINDERS: 480 × 600mm
COUPLED WHEELS: 1210mm
GRATE AREA: 1.7m^2
BOILER PRESSURE: 12kg/cm^2
SUPERHEATED

Narrow Gauge Steam Locomotive Preservation in Sweden

At their zenith, during the second decade of the twentieth century, there were about 180 private railways operating in Sweden. On nearly all of them, steam locomotives provided the motive power and a large proportion of these railways were of narrow gauge.

The principal narrow gauge lines were laid to a gauge of 891mm which was 3 Swedish feet, and these lines accounted for about 20 per cent of the total railway route kilometrage in Sweden. Next in importance, in the narrow gauge field, were the 600mm-gauge lines. The larger 1067mm gauge was also well represented and there were a few railways of which the gauge was 802mm and others of 1093mm.

A considerable number of narrow gauge steam locomotives has been preserved and each of the five gauges is represented. Many of these locomotives are kept, in various states of repair, in public parks and children's playgrounds, but others have found more dignified and secure retirement in museums, including the Railway Museum at Gävle.

Sweden has many practical locomotive enthusiasts and they have, for some time, been successfully operating steam locomotives on narrow gauge railways as tourist attractions. The most important of these are:

(i) *Östra Sodermanlands Järnväg* (*ÖSlJ*) which operates a former SJ14.35mm-gauge line between Mariefred on Lake Mälaren and Laggesta East. The railway was converted to 600mm gauge by *OSlJ*. As many as nine trains each way each day may be run on summer Sundays. This line opened for traffic in July 1966 but much of the equipment had previously been used over a brick works line at Sodertalje.

(ii) *Stora Lundby Järnvägsmuseum* (*StLyJ*). This society was founded in 1965 for the purpose of preserving and operating 891mm-gauge steam locomotives and rolling stock. It is particularly interested in the former Västergötland Göteborgs Railway (VGJ) which was nationalised to become part of SJ in 1948. StLyJ has been allowed by SJ to operate trains over the VGJ tracks several times a year but, in 1967, SJ decided to close the VGJ line. This has been done in sections at different times but from August 1970 all passenger traffic throughout the 121km from Sjövik to Forshem has ceased and only a short section retained for freight traffic. However, StLyJ has been able to rent from SJ, as from October, 1970, the 12km section between Anten and Gräfsnäs, and four or five trains each way will be operated on Sundays during summer. This section will be isolated from all other rail connections by lifting of the track between Gräfsnäs and Sollebrunn.

(iii) *Järnvägarnas Museisallskap* operate an 891-mm-gauge industrial line between Jadraas and Tallas.

(iv) *Stockholm Roslagens Järnväg* own several locomotives which they will operate over the 891mm-gauge line between Rimbo and Syninge.

The locomotives which work on these railways are described in the following pages.

ÖSIJ No 1 LOTTA   [ÖSIJ

No 1 *LOTTA* is an outside-cylinder 0–4–0 Well Tank locomotive built in 1913 by Orenstein and Koppel (works number 6620) for SJ Central Building Depot.

SJ used it for construction work and it was then sold to Kohlswa Ironworks. Later it went to work at the Kohlswa felspar mine at Torp but when this mine was closed, it was locked away in a shed and, presumably, forgotten.

Prospecting for uranium in the district brought the existence of the little locomotive to the attention of the Swedish Locomotive Club but enquiries made of the Kolswar Ironworks failed to find any reference to the locomotive. The Company agreed, however, to give the locomotive to ÖSIJ. It was named *LOTTA* and numbered 2. It went to work on the original "museum railway" at Lina Bruk near Södertalje and was moved to Mariefred in 1966. It has given excellent service and is easy to maintain. Walschaerts valve gear operates slide valves above the cylinders. It was renumbered 1 so that *VIRA* which was No 2 of the Stafsjö Railway, could retain that number on ÖSlJ.

Dimensions: CYLINDERS: 145 × 260mm
COUPLED WHEELS: 520mm
GRATE AREA: 0.25m²
BOILER PRESSURE: 10kg/cm²

ÖSlJ No 3 DYLTA and train at Mariefred   [K. E. Åkerblom

No 3 *DYLTA* is an 0-4-0 Well Tank locomotive with outside cylinders and Walschaerts valve gear operating slide valves above the cylinders. It was built in 1918 by Orenstein and Koppel (works number 7443) to work at the Åse Limeworks, near Ostersund.

In 1934 it was transferred to Strå Limeworks near Sala and then to the quarries at Dylta north of Örebo. In 1960, these quarries ceased using steam locomotion and No 3 was presented, in immaculate condition, to ÖSlJ arriving at Lina Bruk in 1960.

It had the distinction of working the first train when the ÖSlJ moved to Mariefred.

Dimensions: CYLINDERS: 185 × 300mm
COUPLED WHEELS: 600mm
GRATE AREA: 0.35m^2
BOILER PRESSURE: 12kg/cm^2

ÖSlJ No 6 SMEDJEBACKEN [K. E. Åkerblom

No 6 *SMEDJEBACKEN* is an outside-cylinder 0–4–0 Well Tank locomotive which was built in 1929 by Orenstein and Koppel (works number
11970) for the Smedjebacken Rolling Mills in Västmanland.

There was a considerable network of 600mm-gauge railway within these
rolling mills and, at one time, nine steam locomotives were on the roster.
In 1951, steam was replaced by diesel power but No 6 was saved from the
scrap-heap and, after being overhauled and painted by the Works'
apprentices, it went to the ÖSlJ arriving at Mariefred in 1967.

No 6 has not yet been put to work on the ÖSlJ.

Dimensions: NOT KNOWN, BUT SIMILAR TO NO 3.

ÖSlJ No 7 HELGENÄS as first built

ÖSlJ No 7 HELGENÄS as delivered to Mariefred   [K. E. Åkerblom

No 7 *HELGENÄS* is an 0–4–2 Saddle Tank locomotive built in 1889 by Hudswell Clark (works number 346). It worked on a short line between Edsbenk and Hälgenäs Harbour on the Baltic Coast. As built, it had a rather ineffective spark arrester at the chimney top and this was replaced by one of the standard Swedish pattern at the base of the chimney.

In 1965, No 7 was presented to ÖSlJ and has since been largely rebuilt by students of the School of Engineering at Eskilstuna, drawings being obtained from the builders in England. The original boiler barrel was used, but smokebox, tubes and tube plates were renewed. The locomotive was again in steam in 1970.

Dimensions: CYLINDERS: 190 × 305mm
COUPLED WHEELS: 610mm
BOILER PRESSURE: 8kg/cm^2

SWEDEN   2–4–2T   600mm
Östra Sodermanlands Järnväg (ÖSlJ)

ÖSlJ No 2 VIRÅ   [K. E. Åkerblom

No 2 *VIRÅ* is an outside-cylinder 2–4–2 Side Tank locomotive built in 1901 by Motala (works number 272) for the Stafsjö Railway in Kolmården as their No 2.

This railway had been built to clear an insect-damaged forest and to transport the timber to a harbour nearby. This line also became quite well patronised for passenger traffic until, as a result of World War I, the railway was in debt and No 2 was sold to the Bjørkåsen Mines in Northern Norway. The locomotive was found in good condition by representatives of ÖSlJ and, on the closure of the mine in 1965, it was presented to the railway by the owners of the mine. It was the first locomotive at Mariefred.

It was completely overhauled and went into regular service for ÖSlJ in 1967 and has been a reliable and economical unit ever since. It has a Swedish-type spark arrester at the base of the chimney. The coupled wheels are inside the frames with outside cranks, and Allan link motion.

Dimensions: CYLINDERS: 190 × 280mm
              COUPLED WHEELS: 600mm
              GRATE AREA: 0.36m²
              BOILER PRESSURE: 12kg/cm²

SWEDEN   2–6–2T   600mm
Östra Sodermanlands Järnväg (ÖSlJ)

ÖSlJ No 4 K.M.NELSSON   [K. E. Åkerblom

No 4 *K.M.NELSSON* is a superheated 2–6–2 Side Tank locomotive with the coupled wheel inside the frames but cranks and motion, outside. Two sets of Walschaerts valve gear operate piston valves above the cylinders. The locomotive was built in 1914 by Motala (works number 520) for the Nättraby-Alnaryd-Älmeboda Railway (NAAJ). This railway was closed in 1939.

In 1946, No 4 was bought by Aspa Bruk and, with a similar engine, was used to work timber trains on a 15km-long 600mm-gauge railway. Steam working on this line stopped in 1955 and the locomotives were stored for emergency reserve. ÖSlJ was promised these locomotives when they became available but, in the event, they went to two different museums in 1963. Ultimately, No 4 was exchanged for a 1435mm-gauge industrial tank locomotive and it arrived at Läggesta in 1967. It is at present stored, awaiting complete overhaul.

Dimensions: CYLINDERS: 260 × 280mm
               COUPLED WHEELS: 600mm
               GRATE AREA: 0.48m^2
               BOILER PRESSURE: 12kg/cm^2
               SUPERHEATED

SWEDEN   0–8–0T   600mm
Östra Sodermanlands Järnväg (ÖSIJ)

ÖSIJ No 8 EMSFORS   [L. Welander

No 8 *EMSFORS* is an 0–8–0 Side Tank locomotive with outside frames and outside cylinders having slide valves on top of the cylinders and actuated by Stephenson link motion. It was built in 1919 by Chemnitz (works number 4290) and was one of two bought by the Emsfors Paper Mills to operate their 3km-long line between the Mills and the Baltic Coast at Påskallvik.

These locomotives were built to a standard German design for Feldbahn locomotives during World War I. Provision was made for some radial and lateral movement of the first and fourth axles on irregular and severely curved track.

No 8 is now in reserve at Emsfors having been replaced by a diesel locomotive. It will go to ÖSIJ in the near future and will be a powerful addition to the motive power roster of that railway.

Dimensions: CYLINDERS: 240 × 240mm
            COUPLED WHEELS: 600mm
            GRATE AREA: 0.42m²
            BOILER PRESSURE: 13 kg/cm²

SWEDEN   0–4–4–0T   600mm
Östra Sodermanlands Järnväg (ÖSlJ)

ÖSlJ No 4 HAMRA   [ÖSlJ

No 5 *HAMRA* is a Mallet four-cylinder compound 0–4–4–0 Side Tank locomotive which was built in 1902 by Orenstein and Koppel (works number 930) for the Hamra Railway at Tumba south of Stockholm.

This locomotive worked between a number of industrial sites including a paper mill, a research farm and a gravel pit, hauling their products to the SJ line at Tumba. The line was closed in 1947 and the engine went to a lime quarry on the Island of Gotland. After working there for ten years, No 5 was due to be scrapped but was saved by the Swedish Railway Club who exchanged it for their No 1 *BLIXTEN* (obtained from Smedjebacken Rolling Mills), a worn-out tank locomotive of equivalent scrap value!

No 5 underwent complete overhaul from 1961 to 1964 and later, after the removal of the ÖSlJ to Mariefred, the boiler was again renovated. In 1969 it went into regular service on the ÖSlJ.

Steam distribution for both high pressure and low pressure cylinders is by slide valves operated by Hackworth valve gear.

Dimensions: CYLINDERS: HIGH PRESSURE: 195 × 260mm
                              LOW PRESSURE: 295 × 260mm
           COUPLED WHEELS: 545mm
           GRATE AREA: 0.5m^2
           BOILER PRESSURE: 10kg/cm^2

SWEDEN   0–4–0T   600mm

No 10 is an outside-cylinder 0–4–0 Well Tank locomotive which was built in 1913 by Orenstein and Koppel (works number 6619) for Byggnadscentral Förrådet (SJ Central Workshops).

It is to be preserved in the Railway Museum at Gävle.

Dimensions: CYLINDERS: 150 × 275mm
                COUPLED WHEELS: 550mm
                GRATE AREA: 0.25m^2
                BOILER PRESSURE: 12kg/cm^2

No 9 is an outside-cylinder 2–6–2 Side Tank locomotive which was built in 1915 by Motala (works number 568) for the Jönköping Gripenberg Railway (JGJ). In 1935 it went to Munksjo AB, Aspa Bruk, as their No 4 and in 1963 was sent for preservation to the Skärstad Museum.

Dimensions: NOT KNOWN

SWEDEN   0–4–4–0T   600mm

KLJ No 2 now named LESSEBO   [Railway Museum SJ

No 2 *LESSEBO* is a Mallet four-cylinder compound 0–4–4–0 Side Tank
locomotive which was built in 1891 by Munktells (works number 27) for
the Kosta Lessebo Railway (KLJ). It is now preserved in the Railway
Museum at Gävle.

This locomotive was sold by KLJ to Munkedals AB and became their
No 6. For many years it carried the name *A. MALLET*.

The first Mallet engine ever built was constructed in 1887 at Ateliers
Metallurgiques in Tubize, Belgium and was used on a 600mm-gauge
Decauville line. It was very successful and during the next few years, a
considerable number of exactly similar engines was built for several
countries, all for the 600mm-gauge. This Swedish locomotive was built
under licence but is an excellent example of the type. Not all, however,
had such large spark arresters on the chimney.

Dimensions: CYLINDERS: HIGH PRESSURE: 187 × 260mm
                             LOW PRESSURE: 280 × 260mm
              COUPLED WHEELS: 600mm
              GRATE AREA: 0.51m^2
              BOILER PRESSURE: 12kg/cm^2

WMJ No 4   [L. O. Karlsson

No 4 is an outside-cylinder 2–6–0 Side Tank locomotive which was built
in 1887 by Nydquist (works number 249) for the Wikern Möckelns
Railway (WMJ). It then went to the Nora Bergslags Railway (NBsJ)
until finally being owned by the Bredsjö Degerfors Railway (BDJ). It
was withdrawn and, in 1956, was put on exhibition in the open at Nora
Station.

No 4 has a round-top boiler surmounted by two ornamental domes,
the first of which is for sand. A large Swedish-type spark arrester is at
the base of the chimney. The main technical interest in this locomotive
is that it has an early form of Joy's valve gear, a form which was designed
for outside cylinder locomotives. The connecting and anchor links of the
valve gear are modified and a return crank provides motion to one end
of the anchor link. In No 4, the cylinders are horizontal with slide valves
above them.

Dimensions: NOT KNOWN

186

SVJ No 4 SEBASTIAN GRAVE   [Railway Museum SJ

No 4 *SEBASTIAN GRAVE*, is an outside-cylinder 0–6–4 Side Tank locomotive which was built in 1883 by Kristinehamn (works number 29) for the Säfsnäs Verkens Railway (SVJ). It was withdrawn and preserved in the Railway Museum in 1953 and is now at Gävle.

This rather odd-looking locomotive has several interesting features. The coupled wheelbase has been kept very short, the coupled wheels being as close together as possible; the trailing coupled wheels are well forward of the firebox. The drive from the cylinders is to the third coupled axle, outside Stephenson link motion operating the slide valves inclined above the cylinders. The trailing bogie also has a very short wheelbase, both axles being beneath the footplate and well behind the firebox. The boiler is surmounted by an ornamental dome and the round-top firebox is much higher than the boiler barrel. The locomotive weighs only 17.5 tonnes in working order.

Dimensions: CYLINDERS: 280 × 386mm
COUPLED WHEELS: 760mm
GRATE AREA: 0.71m²
BOILER PRESSURE: 9kg/cm²

187

SWEDEN   2–8–2T   802mm

No 7 *KNUT FALK* is an outside-cylinder 2–8–2 Side Tank locomotive with a superheater boiler and piston valves operated by Walschaerts valve gear. It was built in 1920 by Helsingborg (works number 59) for the Säfsnäs Verkens Railway (SVJ). It was later owned by the Hällefors Frederiksbergs Railway (HFJ) and is now preserved in the *Fredriksdals Friluftmuseum* at Hälsingborg.

Dimensions: NOT KNOWN

StLyJ No 31   [L. O. Karlsson

No 31 is an outside-cylinder 4–6–0 locomotive with six-wheel tender. This locomotive was built in 1941 by Henschel (works number 25935) for the Västergötland Göteborg Railway (VGJ).

In 1949 VGJ was taken over by SJ and No 31 became SJ No 3110 of Class B4p. It is now in good running order and has been given its original VGJ number. It is an elegant and powerful unit in StLyJ roster.

In appearance, No 31 is not unlike a smaller edition of the SJ 4–6–0 of Class B for the 1435mm gauge. The cab is enclosed and has a "wind-cutter" front. A turbo-generator behind the chimney supplies electricity for lighting: there is a massive headlight in front of the chimney.

The engine has a round-top boiler with superheater and outside Walschaerts gear operates piston valves above the cylinders.

Dimensions: CYLINDERS: 370 × 500mm
  COUPLED WHEELS: 1300mm
  GRATE AREA: 1.5m^2
  BOILER PRESSURE: 13.5kg/cm^2
  SUPERHEATED

StLyJ No 24 [L. O. Karlsson

No 24 is an outside-cylinder 4–6–0 locomotive with four-wheel tender which was built in 1911 by Nydquist (works number 982) for the Västergötland Göteborg Railway. In 1949, it became SJ No 3105 of Class B2p. Now in working order and in service on StLyJ, it has had its original number restored.

No 24 is a smaller and much older engine than No 31 but has a superheated round top boiler and piston valves above the cylinders operated by Walschaerts valve gear.

Dimensions: CYLINDERS: 370 × 500mm
COUPLED WHEELS: 1300mm
GRATE AREA: 1.0m²
BOILER PRESSURE: 12kg/cm²
SUPERHEATED

SWEDEN   0–4–0T   891mm
Stora Lundby Museum Railway (StLyJ)

StLyJ GÖTA I   [StLyJ

GÖTA I is a diminutive 0–4–0 Well Tank locomotive built in 1906 by Orenstein and Koppel (works number 1611) for an industrial concern in Göta.

Its overall length is only 4150mm and weight in working order only 8 tonnes, but it has a large spark arresting chimney and an even larger cab! Slide valves, operated by outside Hackworth valve gear, are above the cylinders.

This locomotive, now the property of Stora Lundby Järnvägs Museum, is not in working order and will be retained as a museum piece.

Dimensions: NOT KNOWN

StLyJ No 5 NANNA   [StLyJ]

No 5 is an outside-cylinder 4–4–0 Side Tank locomotive which was built
in 1897 by Nydquist (works number 464) for the Kalmar Berga Railway
(KBJ) on which it was No 5 *NANNA*. It later became No 35 (un-named)
of the Stockholm Rimbo Railway (SRJ). It is now owned by StLyJ but
is not in working order and may be retained only as a museum exhibit.

This little engine has a Swedish type spark arrester. The cylinders,
with slide valves on top, are located between the bogie wheels and the
drive is to the leading coupled wheels. The valve gear is Allan link
motion.

Dimensions: CYLINDERS: 335 × 460mm
              COUPLED WHEELS: 1220mm
              BOILER PRESSURE: 9kg/cm²

SWEDEN 2–6–0T 891mm
Stora Lundby Museum Railway (StLyJ)

StLyJ No 3 as SJ No 3026 [StLyJ]

No 3 is an outside-cylinder 2–6–0 Side Tank locomotive which was built in 1910 by Nydquist (works number 951) for the Ruda Ostershamns Railway (ROJ). This railway later changed its name to Östra Småland Railway (ÖSmJ), but the locomotive numbers remained the same.

In 1940, ÖSmJ was taken over by SJ and No 3 became No 3026 of Class S9p. It was withdrawn in 1959. In the ownership of StLyJ, this engine has reverted to No 3 of ROJ. It has been completely overhauled and is again in traffic.

Dimensions: CYLINDERS: 350 × 460mm
    COUPLED WHEELS: 1010mm
    GRATE AREA: 0.8m²
    BOILER PRESSURE: 10kg/cm²

StLyJ No 6   [StLyJ]

No 6 is an outside-cylinder 2–8–0 Side Tank locomotive which was built in 1916 by Motala (works number 566) for the Byvalla Långshyttan Railway (BLJ). It is now owned by *Stora Lundby Järnvägsmuseum* by whom it will be operated. It is at present under repair.

Although of an unusual tank engine type, this is a modern and handsome little engine. A round-top superheated boiler supplies steam to two outside cylinders with piston valves which are operated by Walschaerts valve gear. A small turbo generator provides power for electric lighting.

Dimensions: CYLINDERS: 360 × 460mm

            COUPLED WHEELS: 950mm

            GRATE AREA: 1.0m^2

            BOILER PRESSURE: 11kg/cm^2

            SUPERHEATED

SWEDEN   2–6–0   891mm

No 22 is an outside-cylinder 2–6–0 locomotive built for the Hultsfred Västervik Railway (HVJ) in 1907 by Nydquist (works number 848). It then went to the Norsholm Västervik Hultsfred Railway (NVHJ) and, in 1949, became SJ No 3147 Class L18p. It is to be preserved at Kulbacken, Västervik.

Dimensions: NOT KNOWN

SRJ 2–6–2 No 28 [Railway Museum SJ

No 28 is a modern outside-cylinder 2–6–2 locomotive with a bogie tender. It was built in 1920 by Henschel (works number 17607) for the Stockholm Rimbo Railway (SRJ) and it is now preserved in the Railway Museum at Gävle.

This is the survivor of a class of locomotives which superseded two-cylinder compound 2–6–0s on the SRJ main line. It has a round-top superheated boiler with the steam dome and sand dome under the same cover. Piston valves above the cylinders are operated by Walschaerts valve gear. The leading wheels are in a Bissel truck but the trailing radial wheels are inside a backward extension of the main frames. They are provided with radial axle boxes which allow considerable lateral movement.

Dimensions: CYLINDERS: 420 × 600mm
COUPLED WHEELS: 1300mm
GRATE AREA: 1.60m²
BOILER PRESSURE: 13kg/cm²
SUPERHEATED

BLJ 2–8–0 No 5 THOR   [L. O. Karlsson

No 5 *THOR* is an outside-cylinder 2–8–0 locomotive built in 1909 by Falun (works number 107) for the Byvalla Långshyttan Railway (BLJ) which no longer exists. No. 5 is exhibited in the open in the childrens playground at Långshyttan.

This is a freight locomotive with a Belpaire boiler. The slide valves above the cylinders are operated by Walschaerts valve gear. The tender is four-wheeled.

Dimensions: NOT KNOWN

SJ 2–8–0 No 3119 [L. O. Karlsson]

SJ No 3119 Class Gp is a superheated outside-cylinder 2–8–0 locomotive with piston valves operated by Walschaerts valve gear. It was built in 1937 by Motala (works number 836) for the Västergötland Göteborg Railway (VGJ) as their No 29. It is at present exhibited in a children's playground at Skara.

A modern locomotive with round-top boiler and a totally enclosed cab. A four-wheeled tender is attached.

SJ No 3132 Class Gp is a similar locomotive to No 3119 (above) but was built for SJ in 1950 by Motala (works number 969).

It is at present located at Ösby, *Stockholm Roslagens Museiforening*.
Dimensions: NOT KNOWN

DONJ Mallet No 12   [L. O. Karlsson

No 12 is a Mallet four-cylinder compound 0–6–6–0 locomotive which was built in 1910 by AB Atlas, Stockholm (works number 114) for the Dala Ockelbo Norrsundets Railway (DONJ). It is to go to the Railway Museum at Gävle.

No 12 was one of three Mallet locomotives which were built for DONJ and they were the largest and most powerful of their type in Sweden. DONJ dealt with heavy timber traffic which No 12 and her sisters handled successfully for more than 50 years.

The design incorporates a round-top boiler with, later, the sand box for the rear coupled wheels and the steam dome in the same cover. The sand box for the leading coupled wheels is in the form of a saddle on top of the smokebox in front of the chimney. Above both high pressure and low pressure cylinders are slide valves actuated by Walschaerts valve gear.

Dimensions: CYLINDERS: HIGH PRESSURE: 330 × 500mm
 LOW PRESSURE: 500 × 500mm
  COUPLED WHEELS: 1000mm
  GRATE AREA: 1.7m²
  BOILER PRESSURE: 12kg/cm²

No I UA is an 0–4–2 Tank locomotive which was built in 1871 by Henry Hughes, Falcon Works, Loughborough, England, for Nordmark Klarälvens Railway (NKlJ). It is preserved and on exhibition at the railway station at Hagfors.

No other details are available.

SRJ No 3 RIMBO   [Brian Garvin

No 3 *RIMBO* is an outside-cylinder 2–4–0 Well Tank locomotive built in 1884 by Nydquist (works number 195) for the Stockholm Rimbo Railway (SRJ). It is preserved in the Railway Museum at Gävle.

This is quite a handsome and well-proportioned little engine with a round-top boiler, polished brass dome cover and Salter type safety valves. A Swedish type spark arrester is at the base of the chimney. Slide valves, inclined forwards above the cylinders are operated by outside Allan link motion.

Dimensions: CYLINDERS: 290 × 400mm
           COUPLED WHEELS: 1000mm
           GRATE AREA: 0.68m²
           BOILER PRESSURE: 10kg/cm²

BLJ No 9   [L. O. Karlsson

No 9 is an outside-cylinder 2–4–0 Side Tank locomotive which was built in 1898 by Motala (works number 196) for the Mariestad Kinnekulle Railway (MKlJ) as their No 2. In 1909 it was sold to the Västergötland Göteborg Railway (VGJ) who again sold it, in 1941, to its final owners, the Byvalla Långshyttan Railway (BLJ). It is now preserved, in working order, by the *Järnvägarnas Museisällskap* at Jädraås.

There are several features of interest in this little locomotive. Those parts of the "side tanks" nearest the cab are, in fact, coal bunkers and water is carried only in their forward parts. The sand box is mounted in the form of a saddle across the boiler in front of the dome. The boiler has a Belpaire firebox and the safety valve is on top of the dome. Slide valves, above the cylinders, are operated by outside Allan link motion.

Dimensions: NOT KNOWN

No 1 *STEN STURE* is an o–6–o Side Tank locomotive built as an o–6–o Saddle Tank locomotive in 1873 by Fletcher Jennings (works number 119) for the Ulricehamn Railway (UJ). It was sold in 1907 to Falköping Uddagårdens Railway (FUJ) and converted to its present form. In 1955 it was transferred as a museum piece to *Yxhults Stennhugger AB* where it remains as a monument.

Dimensions: NOT KNOWN

GJ No 3 GOTLAND   [Railway Museum SJ

No 3 *GOTLAND* is an outside-cylinder o–6–o Side Tank locomotive, built in 1878 by Nydquist (works number 89) for the Gotlands Railway (GJ). In 1948 it was taken over by SJ and became their No 3063 Class K2p. It was withdrawn in 1955 and has now been restored to its original condition and is preserved in the Railway Museum at Gävle.

This little engine has a Belpaire boiler and the safety valves of the Salter Type are on the dome. Slide valves above the cylinders are operated by outside Allan link motion. It has hand-operated brakes with wooden brake blocks.

Dimensions: CYLINDERS: 280 × 406mm
               COUPLED WHEELS: 990mm
               GRATE AREA: 0.58m^2
               BOILER PRESSURE: 10kg/cm^2

The following are 0–6–0 Tank locomotives for 891mm gauge and which are preserved. Details about them are incomplete.
No 2 *KLOSTER* is an outside-cylinder 0–6–0 Tank locomotive which was built in 1890 by Nohab (works number 303) for the Byvalla Långshyttan Railway (BLJ). It is now preserved as a monument in the children's playground (*Bangården*) at Långshyttan.

SJ No 3067 class K4p is an 0–6–0 Side Tank locomotive with outside cylinders which was built in 1897 by Kristinehamn (works number 59) for the Klintehamn Roma Railway (KlRJ) as their No 1 *KLINTEHAMN*. This locomotive was transferred to SJ and renumbered in 1948. It is at present preserved at Målilla

HvSJ No 4 A.WILH.PETRI   [L. O. Karlsson

No 4 *A.WILH.PETRI* is an outside-cylinder Side Tank locomotive which was built in 1900 by Motala (works number 239) for the Hvetlanda Sävsjö Railway (HvSJ). It later became Hvetlanda Railway (HvJ) No 4 and, from about 1946, was SJ No 3048 Class Kp. It has been restored to its original condition and, with two four-wheeled coaches, is exhibited in Hembygdsparken at Nassjo.

No 5 *LOVISA TRANÆA* is an 0–6–0 Tank locomotive which was built in 1875 by Avonside (works number 1117) for the Nordmark Klarälvens Railway (NKlJ). This locomotive is preserved as a monument at Hagfors station.

SJ No 3094 Class S5p

[L. O. Karlsson]

SJ No 3094 Class S5p is an outside-cylinder 2–6–0 Side Tank locomotive which was built in 1899 by Motala (works number 193) for the Västergötland Göteborg Railway (VGJ) as their No 4. It was taken over by SJ in (about) 1949 and is now preserved as a monument in the Gamla Children's Playground (*Bangården*) at Hjo.

This locomotive is preserved in its final condition and with its SJ number. The steam dome and the sand dome are within the same cover. Slide valves, inclined above the cylinders, are operated by outside Allan link motion. The cab is totally enclosed.

Dimensions: NOT KNOWN

Industrial 0–6–2WT No 2 KORSÅN [L. O. Karlsson

No 2 *KORSÅN* is an outside-cylinder 0–6–2 Well Tank locomotive which was built in 1902 by Falun (works number 21) for the industrial firm Stora Kopparberge Bergslags AB, Vintjärn Åg Hinsen Railway. This locomotive was built as an 0–6–0WT, but was later rebuilt as an 0–6–2WT with a larger cab and a coal bunker behind the cab. Slide valves above the cylinders are operated by Walschaerts valve gear.

This locomotive is preserved in working order by Järnvägarnas Museisällskap, Jädraäs.

Dimensions: NOT KNOWN

SWEDEN   2–6–2T   891mm

SJ No 3037 Class S2p is a 2–6–2 Side Tank locomotive with outside cylinders and Walschaerts valve gear. It was built in 1919 for the Kalmar Torsås Railway (KTsJ) as their No 15 and was taken over by SJ in, about, 1941. The builder was Kalmar and it was works number 1 of that firm.

It is preserved as a monument in a public park in Kalmar.

Dimensions: NOT KNOWN

SWEDEN   2–8–0T   891mm

No 6 is an outside-cylinder 2–8–0 Side Tank locomotive, built in 1920 by Motala (works number 664) for the Södra Ölands Railway (SÖJ). It later became the property of the Ölands Railway (ÖJ) before being taken over by *Statens Järnväger* (SJ) in 1947 when it became No 3050 of Class Np.

It has been restored to its original number and placed on display in the Gamla *Bangården* (children's playground) at Borgholm.

Dimensions: NOT KNOWN

SJ 3178 as a children's plaything   [L. O. Karlsson

SJ No 3178 Class Np is an outside-cylinder 2–8–0 Side Tank locomotive which was built in 1918 as No 24 for the Nordmark Klarälvens Railway (NKlJ) by Motala (works number 637).

The round-top superheated boiler is surmounted by two domes, the first being the sand dome. Walschaerts valve gear operates piston valves and a small amount of lateral movement is provided in the trailing axle.

This locomotive exists as a plaything for children at Västra Frölunda. It is surrounded and surmounted by guard rails and it shows many

209

"bruises" caused by the boots of young climbers! Rather a sad end for a fine little engine.

Dimensions: NOT KNOWN

SJ No 3073 Class N5p is a 2–8–0 Side Tank locomotive with outside cylinders and piston valves operated by Walschaerts valve gear. It was built for the Slite Roma Railway (SlRJ) as their No 3 in 1920 by Henschel (works number 18152). It is now preserved as a monument in a children's playground at Roma.

Dimensions: NOT KNOWN

NÖJ No 18   [R. G. Farr

No 18 is an outside-cylinder 2–8–2 Side Tank locomotive with a round-top superheater boiler and with piston valves operated by Walschaerts valve gear. The drive is to the third coupled axle.

This locomotive was built in 1921 by Motala (works number 668) for the Norra Östergötland Railway (NÖJ). It was taken over by SJ in, about, 1950 to become their No 3160 Class N4p. It has had its original number restored and it is to be preserved in the museum at Linköping.

Dimensions: NOT KNOWN

SJ No 4013 Class L2t

[L. O. Karlsson

No 9 is an outside-cylinder 2–6–0 locomotive which was built for the Blekinge Coast Railway, *Blekinge Kustbanor* (BKB) in 1907 by Nydquist (works number 836). It became SJ No 4013 Class L2t in 1942 and is now in store at Upsala SJ Depot before going to the Railway Museum at Gävle.

This is a useful little engine with a short coupled wheelbase. It is superheated and has piston valves operated by Walschaerts valve gear. The sandbox and steam dome are within the same casing and a small turbo-generator set supplies current for lighting. The tender has four wheels only.

Dimensions: CYLINDERS: 400 × 500mm

           COUPLED WHEELS: 1170mm

           GRATE AREA: 1.0m^2

           BOILER PRESSURE: 10kg/cm^2

           SUPERHEATED

SJ No 4006 Class W4t is an outside-cylinder 4–4–0 Side Tank locomotive built in 1901 by Nohab (works number 625) for the Västra Blekinge Railway (WBlJ) as their No 19. It became Blekinge Coast Railway (BKB) in 1905 retaining the same number. In 1949 it was taken over by SJ.

This locomotive is preserved in the museum at Kristianstad.

Dimensions: NOT KNOWN

SWEDEN   0–6–0T   1093mm

No 7 *PATRIC REUTERSWARD* is an outside-cylinder 0–6–0 Tank locomotive which was built in 1894 by Nohab (works number 390) for the Köping Uttersberg Railway (KUJ). It is to be preserved in the museum at Köping.

No further details are available.

Swiss Federal Railways

The Swiss Federal Railways, *Schweizerische Bundesbahnen* (SBB) were
formed by an amalgamation, in 1902, of the five largest private railways
and their associate companies.

The total railway route kilometrage in Switzerland is about 5,200km
not including tramways and pure rack mountain railways. Of this total,
SBB operate some 2,840km of 1435mm gauge, mostly double track.
About 800km of 1435mm gauge railway, mostly single track, is operated
by 36 private companies, many of which have amalgamated.

With the exception of 22km of diesel-operated railway, all the 1435mm
gauge railways are electrified, nearly all using 15,000 volts, $16\frac{2}{3}$ cycle,
single phase, alternating current. Most of the railways began by being
steam operated and, over the years, the steady progress of electrification
has resulted in the replacement of steam locomotives, some of which have
been preserved. These are described in the pages which follow. Mention
is also made of the many locomotives which have been sold by railway
companies and the SBB to Industrial Companies in Switzerland and
which are still at work. It is likely that some of these will be preserved
and placed on display in the future.

Locomotive Preservation in Switzerland

The principal collection of preserved locomotives is to be found in the
Verkehrshaus der Schweiz at Lucerne. This excellently laid-out museum is
one of the best of its kind in Europe and presents, not only railways, but
also all means of communication by sea, land, air and by telephone. The
railway section contains many original locomotives, some of which are
displayed in the open. Interesting electric as well as steam locomotives
are shown and there is a number of excellent large-scale models.
Noteworthy is the fine scenic working model of the Gotthard Railway.

A number of interesting standard gauge steam (and other) locomotives
is kept in store in the SBB Depot at Vallorbe. Four of these at a time
are placed on exhibition outside the *Verkehrshaus* during the spring and
summer of each year. A different group of four locomotives is sent from
Vallorbe each succeeding year until, in rotation, all have been
exhibited. A special switch has been inserted in the SBB line which
passes close to the *Verkehrshaus* and a portable track has been constructed to
lay temporarily across the intervening highway. The tracks in the
Verkehrshaus grounds can thus be directly connected with the main SBB
lines.

Another technical museum which at present is in course of preparation
and construction is *Technorama* at Winterthur. Much material of the
greatest interest has been accumulated but is at present stored in what
will ultimately become one of the museum halls. At present there are

two steam locomotives in the collection, but *Technorama* is to be a museum of engineering and industry and not a museum of transport.

In Switzerland many steam locomotives are on display in children's playgrounds and public parks while others are preserved in working order and are used from time to time to work special trains. There are also some locomotives which have been privately preserved, including two express locomotives of the SNCF and one from DB.

Although small in number, the Swiss locomotive enthusiasts have done a fine job in preserving much of their country's transport heritage.

N–O–B 4–2–0 No 1 LIMMAT in the Verkehrshaus, Lucerne (full-scale working model) [P. R-W

In the *Verkehrshaus de Schweiz* at Lucerne one of the most attractive exhibits is a full-size working model of the North Eastern Railway (N-O-B) 4–2–0 locomotive No 1 named *LIMMAT*. The original engine was one of two built by Emil Kessler, works number 78, in Kalrsruhe in 1847 for the Northern Railway. The *Spanisch-Brötli-Bahn* which ran between Zürich and Baden and was so called because it quickly delivered to the people of Zürich a much loved Baden delicacy, the "Spanish bun"! The locomotive was withdrawn in 1882 having been rebuilt and reboilered in 1866.

The present exhibit was built by SLM in 1947 for the Swiss Railway Centenary celebrations and is their works number 3937 of 1947.

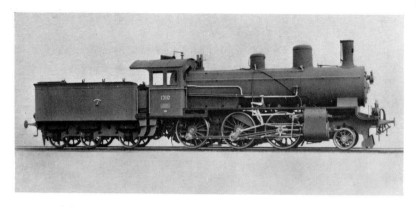

SBB 2–6–0 No 1310 was a sister engine of the preserved locomotive No 1367   [SBB

No 1367 (SLM 2557/16) is stored at Vallorbe, scheduled for preservation in the *Verkehrshaus* at Lucerne.

SBB, in 1905, received from SLM the first two of a long series of, then, very modern mixed traffic 2–6–0 locomotives which were Series B 3/4, SBB Group 15.

Though quite small, and classed as *"Personenzuglokomotive"*, they were the first locomotives in Switzerland to be built with superheaters, quite a courageous decision at a time when the advantages of superheated steam were not always fully appreciated. The design was not entirely a successful one as the engines were considerably over-cylindered. The diameter 540mm of the two cylinders was, at that time, more suited to the low pressure side of a compound than to two high pressure cylinders, using superheated steam at 14 atm and distributed by piston valves. As a result of the stresses set up in the motion, driving boxes and frames, the boiler pressure was reduced to 12 atm.

The engines rode exceedingly smoothly, the leading pony wheels and the leading coupled wheels forming a Krauss-Helmholz bogie. In all, 69 of the class were built between 1905 and 1916.

Dimensions: CYLINDERS: 540 × 600mm
COUPLED WHEELS: 1520mm
GRATE AREA: 2.3m^2
BOILER PRESSURE: 12 atm. Superheated
MAXIMUM SPEED: 75km/h

SBB four-cylinder compound 4–6–0 No 760 of the same series as No 705   [P. R-W

SBB No 705 (SLM 1550/04) is stored at Vallorbe and will be preserved in the *Verkehrshaus der Schweiz* at Lucerne. It was withdrawn from service in 1953. In 1954 it received the boiler from No 739 and in 1964, the frames and motion of No 778 during renovation for display.

This elegant locomotive is one of 111 which were built by SLM, between 1902 and 1909. The design was originated by the Jura Simplon Railway and the first two locomotives carried J–S–B numbers 231 and 232, becoming SBB Nos 701 and 702.

The 111 locomotives constituted by far the largest class numerically in Switzerland and they were well liked. They were designed to work trains of 300 tonnes up gradients of 1 in 100 ($10^0/_{00}$) at a steady speed of 50km/h. In practice they were well able to work trains of 400 tonnes to the same requirements.

The locomotives were de Glehn compounds with the high pressure cylinders outside the frames, driving the middle pair of coupled wheels. The low pressure inside cylinders drove the leading coupled wheels and the valve gear for HP and LP was independent.

All the locomotives were built without superheaters but between the years 1913 and 1923, 68 were given Schmidt superheaters, 22 with 21 elements and the remaining 46 engines had 24-element superheaters. Engines Nos 810 and 811 received Brotan boilers in 1907. These were removed in 1913. During that period they carried Nos 651 and 652 respectively.

The locomotives were Series A 3/5 SBB Group 9.

Dimensions: CYLINDERS: HIGH PRESSURE: 360 × 660mm
                   LOW PRESSURE: 570 × 660mm
    COUPLED WHEELS: 1780mm   BOILER PRESSURE: 15 atm
    GRATE AREA: 2.6m²   MAXIMUM SPEED: 100km/h

SBB four-cylinder compound 2–10–0 No 2978 at the Verkehrshaus, Lucerne   [P. R-W

The following SBB four-cylinder compound 2–10–0 locomotives of Series C 5/6 are preserved or are likely to be so:

No 2965 (SLM works number 2518 of 1916), withdrawn 1964, now privately preserved and on display at Erstfeld.

No 2969 (SLM works number 2519 of 1916) is preserved and is on display outside the works of the Swiss Locomotive Company at Winterthur. This locomotive was presented to the City of Winterthur by SBB.

No 2978 (SLM works number 2612 of 1917) is on exhibition outside the *Verkehrshaus* at Lucerne. This locomotive is in the Vallorbe-*Verkehrshaus* "rotation". No 2978 has the boiler from No 2956 and it is in excellent mechanical condition. It will probably be steamed during the 125th Anniversary Celebrations of Swiss railways in 1972.

Thirty 2–10–0 of Series C 5/6 Group 33 locomotives were built by SLM between 1913 and 1917 mainly for freight and heavy passenger services over the Gotthard line. These were the heaviest and most powerful locomotives ever to run in Switzerland, the weight in working order of engine and tender being 128 tonnes and the tractive effort at 85 per cent, 45,000lb. The engines were capable of developing 1,800hp continuously, being designed to work trains of 300 tonnes tare up gradients of 1 in 40 (20⁰/₀₀) at 25km/h.

The first two engines, Nos 2901 and 2902 were four-cylinder simples with the cylinders in line under the smokebox. All the rest of the engines were four-cylinder compounds, again with the cylinders in line and with the high pressure cylinders between the frames and inclined to enable them to drive the second coupled axle. The outside, low pressure cylinders, drove the third coupled axle. There were two sets of Heusinger valve gear. In 1920–22 the two simple engines were rebuilt as compounds and became standard with the rest of the series.

The leading pony truck with the leading coupled axle formed a Krauss-Helmholz bogie of a type modified and improved by SLM.

In 1953, No 2976 was equipped for burning oil fuel and had a large cylindrical oil tank on the tender.

During World War I several of these locomotives with their crews were sent to work on the Paris, Lyons, Mediterranée Railway in France. Their duties consisted of working trains of essential food and fuel into Switzerland, their journeys beginning and ending at Basel.

Dimensions: CYLINDERS: HIGH PRESSURE: 470 × 640mm

LOW PRESSURE: 690 × 640mm

In Nos 2951, 2952 and 2953 the low pressure cylinders were 710mm diameter.

COUPLED WHEELS: 1330mm

GRATE AREA: $3.7m^2$

BOILER PRESSURE: 15atm

SUPERHEATED

Photograph of a model of Bödelibahn No 3 ZEPHIR   [P. R-W

Thunersee Railway (T–S–B) No 72 ex Bödelibahn No 3 (Krauss 290/74) named *ZEPHIR* until recently worked at Metalwerk Dornach as their No 2. It was sold to the company in 1916. It is believed that this locomotive will be preserved but it still works occasionally.

A model of this locomotive is in the *Verkehrshaus*, Lucerne.

Dimensions: CYLINDERS: 225 × 440mm
              COUPLED WHEELS: 800mm
              GRATE AREA: 0.5m²
              BOILER PRESSURE: 12atm

South Eastern Railway (*Sudostbahn*) No 51 (SLM 686/91) was sold to the Kriens-Lucerne Railway in 1896 and in 1912 to St. Gallen Gasworks. It was placed on display in the playground at St. Gallen-Waldau in 1961.

Dimensions: CYLINDERS: 270 × 450mm
              COUPLED WHEELS: 1000mm
              GRATE AREA: 0.5m²
              BOILER PRESSURE: 12atm

The cylinders are on the running plate level with the smokebox and the drive through a rocking lever to the rear coupled axle.

G–B No 11 at the Verkehrshaus, Lucerne   [P. R-W

Gotthard Railway (G-B) No 11 (SLM 236/81) is preserved in the *Verkehrshaus* at Lucerne.

Dimensions: CYLINDERS: 220 × 350mm
  COUPLED WHEELS: 1000mm
  GRATE AREA: 0.4m²
  BOILER PRESSURE: 12atm

The drive and the position of the cylinders are similar to those of S-O-B No 51 described above. No 11, together with a sister engine, No 12, worked postal trains through the Gotthard Tunnel between January and June 1882, being the first locomotives to operate through the tunnel on scheduled services. Despite this distinction, the engines were built for shunting.

J–S–B No 34 was sister-engine of No 35, which is to be preserved   [SBB

Jura Simplon Railway (J-S-B) No 35, SBB No 5469 (Esslingen 2498/91) Type Eb 2/4, SBB Group 47. Preserved and stored for future display in the *Verkehrshaus*, Lucerne.

The J-S-B had 30 4–4–0 passenger tank locomotives for fast light trains. The design originated in 1876 when, between that year and 1888, 20 of the type were built by SLM and Esslingen for the Jura-Berne-Lucerne Railway (J-B-L). This company was absorbed by the J-S-B in 1890 and in 1891–92 ten more of these attractive little engines were built. The cylinders are outside the frames; the drive is to the leading coupled wheels and the valve gear is entirely outside. The safety valves are on the dome.

Dimensions: CYLINDERS: 410 × 612mm
            COUPLED WHEELS: 1555mm
            GRATE AREA: 1.3m^2 (1.4m^2 when reboilered)
            BOILER PRESSURE: 10atm

Engerth Tank locomotive GENF at the Verkehrshaus, Lucerne   [Verkehrshaus der Schweiz

This locomotive, preserved in the *Verkehrshaus* at Lucerne was built in 1858 by Kessler at Esslingen (works number 396) for the Swiss Central Railway (S-C-B). It was their No 28, was named *GENF* and was withdrawn in 1898 having been given a new boiler in 1875.

Dimensions: CYLINDERS: 408 × 561mm
              COUPLED WHEELS: 1375mm
              GRATE AREA: 0.9m²
              BOILER PRESSURE: 9atm as built, 10atm when reboilered

Engerth was a famous Austrian engineer and his "system" involved the utilisation of part of the weight of the loaded tender to add to the adhesive weight of the locomotive. Thus, the rear end of the locomotive was pivotted and this rear end carried coal and some water; the rest of the water was carried in side tanks on the locomotive proper. Engerth locomotives were never built in Britain. They are usually referred to as tank locomotives but, in German, they are referred to as having "stütztenders", i.e. supported tenders. The S-C-B had 60 Engerth locomotives some of which were 0–4–6T, others were 0–4–4T and the remainder 0–6–4T. They were all named and the last four were built in 1872.

Sudostbahn No 4 SCHWYZ   [Sudostbahn

South Eastern Railway (*Sudostbahn*) 0–6–0 Side Tank No 4 *SCHWYZ*, was built at Esslingen in 1887 (works number 2224). It has a domeless boiler (its second).

Dimensions: CYLINDERS: 380 × 530mm
          COUPLED WHEELS: 920mm
          BOILER PRESSURE: 12atm

It was sold in 1941 to Chemie Uetikon and, since 1965, has been on display at Einsiedeln.

SWITZERLAND   1435mm
0–6–0 Well Tank Locomotives

The 0–6–0WT was the standard type of steam shunting locomotive on the SBB and also on most of the private railways of Switzerland, both of those which became part of SBB and of those which remained independent.

The design was developed by the Swiss Locomotive and Machine Company of Winterthur (SLM) who built nearly all the locomotives of this type used in Switzerland, and who supplied the first of them to the Swiss Central Railway in 1873. This order was for ten engines, Nos 81–90, which later became SBB Nos 8580–8589 of Group 83. Dimensions of later engines varied according to the requirements of each railway but the stroke of the two outside cylinders was kept at 500mm in all the engines built.

As electrification made steam locomotives redundant on all the railways, some of these 0–6–0WT were sold to other countries. For example, the Netherlands Railways (NS) in 1945 bought two of the Jura-Simplon series 857–866 of 1901 which became NS Nos 7851 and 7852, while five others of the same series went to Norway in 1947 to become NSB Class 25e.

Many of the redundant locomotives, however, remained in Switzerland where they were bought by various private industrial companies and also by publicly owned enterprises such as gas and water works and the docks management at Basel.

A number of 0–6–0WT is preserved and these are listed here. A much larger number, however, is still at work on industrial railways throughout Switzerland. It is possible that some of these may later be preserved.

E–B No 3 LANGNAU [Fr. Neuenschwander

Emmenthal Railway (E-B) No 3 *LANGNAU* is an o–6–o Well Tank locomotive built in 1881 by SLM (works number 229). It worked for a time for the von Roll Company at Gerlafingen but is now stored at Vallorbe for future preservation in the *Verkehrshaus*. The arrangement of the Walschaerts valve gear is interesting. The eccentric rod from the return crank leads backwards to an expansion link situated under the front of the cab. A very long radius rod meets the combination lever at the level of the leading edge of the second coupled wheel. A long valve rod extends from the combination lever to the slide valve above the cylinder.

Four of these engines were supplied to E-B between 1874 and 1892. The remaining three no longer exist.

Dimensions: CYLINDERS: 340 × 500mm
　　　　　　 COUPLED WHEELS: 1320mm
　　　　　　 GRATE AREA: 1.0m²
　　　　　　 BOILER PRESSURE: 12atm (originally 10atm). New boiler
　　　　　　　　　　　　 fitted in 1909.

North Eastern Railway (*Nordostbahn*) Nos 453–461 were built by SLM, the first five in 1894, the last four in 1896. They became SBB Nos 8551–8559, Series 3/3, Group 80.

Dimensions: CYLINDERS: 350 × 500mm
            COUPLED WHEELS: 1030mm
            GRATE AREA: 0.8m²
            BOILER PRESSURE: 11atm

The weight in W.O. was 27.7 tonnes and maximum speed 40km/h.

NOB 453 (ex 253), SBB No 8551 (SLM 897/94) was sold to Reederei, Basel in 1953 and then carried no number. It was withdrawn in 1963 and placed on display in the playground at Kleinhuningen.

Seetal Railway (S-T-B) No 3 *BEINWYL* (Krauss 1150/84) was sold to Zementfabrik, Wildegg in 1912 and became their No 1. It was retired in 1962 and is now preserved at the playground in Wildegg.

Dimensions: CYLINDERS: 335 × 500mm
            COUPLED WHEELS: 920mm
            BOILER PRESSURE: 12atm

[Sihltalbahn

Sihltal Railway (Sihl-T-B) No 5 was built in 1889 by SLM (works number 1221) is still in the ownership of the railway and is used to haul excursion trains between Zürich (Selnau) and Sihlbrugg during the summer. It will be preserved.

The Sihltalbahn had six 0–6–0WT locomotives built by SLM between 1892 and 1912. Apart from No 5, three others survive:

No 2 SLM works number 795 of 1893 is owned by Basel Gasworks and is said to be sided and awaiting preservation.

No 3 SLM works number 1015 of 1897 is preserved at the *Schule Tannenbach* at Horgen.

No 4 SLM works number 1016 of 1897 is preserved at the *Schule Werd* at Adliswil.

Dimensions varied slightly:

CYLINDERS: diameter Nos 1 and 2: 340mm

,,   ,, 3, 4, 5: 350mm

,,   No 6: 370mm

stroke: 500mm in all engines

COUPLED WHEELS: 1010mm

BOILER PRESSURE: 10atm in Nos 1 and 2

11atm in Nos 3 and 4

12atm in Nos 5 and 6

NO 6 WAS SUPERHEATED

230

G–T–B No 3 as Attisholz No 26   [Dr. Ing. S. Studer

Gürbetal Railway (G-T-B) No 3 is an 0–6–0WT locomotive which was built in 1901 by SLM (works number 1332). It later went to the Thuner-see Railway (T-S-B) as their No 77 and then, in 1926, was owned by the Bern-Lötschberg-Simplon Railway (B-L-S). Finally it was sold to Cellulosefabrik Attisholz and became their works shunter No 26 in which form it is illustrated. It will ultimately be put on display.

Dimensions: CYLINDERS: 360 × 500mm
COUPLED WHEELS: 1030mm
GRATE AREA: 1.2m²
BOILER PRESSURE: 12atm

Swiss Central Railway (S-C-B) No 41 is an 0–6–0WT locomotive which was built in 1901 by SLM (works number 1359). It became SBB No 8410 and, since 1941, has been No 3 of the von Moos Company at Emmen-brücke. It is still at work but will probably be preserved.

Dimensions: CYLINDERS: 340 × 500mm
COUPLED WHEELS: 1030mm
GRATE AREA: 1.1m²
BOILER PRESSURE: 12atm

SBB o–6–oWT No 8487 on display at Buchs [P. R-W

The following Series E 3/3 Group 79 locomotives are known to be preserved or in store awaiting preservation:

No 8487 (SLM works number 1967 of 1909) is on display outside Buchs SBB station.

No 8512 (SLM works number 2135 of 1911) is at Vallorbe and will be exhibited from time to time at the *Verkehrshaus*, Lucerne.

No 8516 (SLM works number 2139 or 1911) has been privately preserved since 1966. This engine was owned by the *Mittelthurgaubahn* from 1963 to 1966 and carried no number.

No 8532 (SLM works number 2544 of 1915) will be put on display at Lyss.

SBB Series E 3/3 Group 79 originated with three outside-cylinder Well Tank locomotives which came from the Swiss Central Railway (S-C-B) when that company became part of SBB in 1902. These locomotives were S-C-B Nos 47–49 (SLM 1456–8/02) and they became SBB Nos 8451–3. Together with the first four o–6–oWT built for the SBB, they had some dimensional differences from the rest of the series, the length over buffers being slightly less and the heating surface was different. All the engines had slide valves above the cylinders and Walschaerts valve gear. The design formed the basis of that for other similar locomotives in several countries.

In all, SBB Group 79 comprised 83 engines numbered 8451–8533 and built over the period 1902–13.

During World War II, coal was extremely scarce in Switzerland and engines Nos 8521 and 8522 were equipped with pantographs on top of the cabs to enable them to collect current to supply electric heating devices which were fitted in the boilers to make steam. The weight of each locomotive was increased by 7 tonnes. The consumption of electric power was enormous.

A number of these locomotives is now owned by industrial firms in Switzerland and are still at work. It is possible that some may be preserved and put on display in public parks or playgrounds.

Dimensions: CYLINDERS: 360 × 500mm
            COUPLED WHEELS: 104mm
            GRATE AREA: 1.17m^2
            BOILER PRESSURE: 12atm

Weight in working order: 34.9 tonnes and maximum speed 45km/h.

H–W–B o–6–oWT No 5 [SLM

Huttwill-Wolhusen Railway (H-W-B) 0–6–0 Well Tank locomotive No 5 is at present used in the Winterthur factory of Sulzer Brothers. It is to be preserved. It was built in 1936 by SLM (works number 3610) and was sold to Sulzer after the electrification of the H-W-B in 1945.

No 5 has piston valves operated by Walschaerts valve gear. The boiler, footplate and bunker are cased-in and the locomotive is designed to be operated from either end by one man. The coal bunker is situated above the firebox-end of the boiler and an automatic stoker obviates the need for a fireman. A feed water pump and pre-heater are also fitted.

This locomotive was a further development of a similar 0–4–0WT supplied to the Langenthal-Huttwill Railway (parent company of the H-W-B) in 1930.

Dimensions: CYLINDERS: 400 × 550mm
COUPLED WHEELS: 1030mm
GRATE AREA: 1.6m^2
BOILER PRESSURE: 13kg/cm^2

234

SWITZERLAND   2–6–0T   1435mm

Saignelegier-Glovelier Railway (R-S-G) No 2 (SLM 1489/03) Series Ed 3/4 became Pruntrut-Bonfol Railway (R-P-B) No 2 in 1934, was withdrawn in 1952 and bought by Sulzer at Oberwinterthur. It is believed to be scheduled for preservation. Identical locomotives were built by SLM for several private railways.

Dimensions: CYLINDERS: 380 × 550mm
                 COUPLED WHEELS: 1030mm
                 GRATE AREA: 1.5m²
                 BOILER PRESSURE: 13atm

Bern-Schwarzenburg Railway (B-S-B) had three locomotives exactly similar to the R-S-G engines above. Of these, No 51 (SLM 1726/06) has worked since 1932 for Zementfabrik Wildegg but is now owned by a group of Bern locomotive enthusiasts.

S–M–B 2–6–0T No 1 Series Ed 3/4   [Fr. Neuenschwander

Solothurn-Munster Railway (S-M-B) Series Ed 3/4 No 1 (SLM 1798/07) was sold to Dreispitz, Basel in 1934 and to Lonza Visp in 1945. It is now said to be scheduled for preservation at Technorama, Winterthur. (This seems doubtful as Technorama is *not* a museum of transport and has no intention, at present, of exhibiting locomotives.)

Dimensions: CYLINDERS: 420 × 600mm
                 COUPLED WHEELS: 1230mm
                 GRATE AREA: 1.7m²
                 BOILER PRESSURE: 12atm

B–T No 9 as SBB No 5889   [SBB

Bodensee-Toggenburg Railway (B-T). Nine 2–6–2T locomotives were built for this line by Maffei in 1910. They were numbered 1–9 Series Eb 3/5 and they became SBB Nos 5881–5889 of Group 53. They were fine-looking machines and were capable of very smart running. All were built with superheaters.

B-T No 6, SBB No 5886 (Maffei 3126/10) has been restored to original condition and, since 1963, has been on display at Degersheim.

B-T No 9, SBB No 5889 (Maffei 3129/10) was restored in 1965 and is now owned by the *Dampflok-Klub* at Herisau.

Dimensions: CYLINDERS: 540 × 600mm
                    COUPLED WHEELS: 1540mm
                    GRATE AREA: 2.4m^2
                    BOILER PRESSURE: 12atm
                    SUPERHEATED

In 1911 the need arose for a powerful tank engine for SBB suburban services and for fast interstation passenger working on country lines which abound in short steep gradients. Following on the success of the B-T engines the 2–6–2T design was adopted and the boiler and motion of the 2–6–0 Series B 3/4 Group 15 were incorporated in the design. The cylinder diameter was, however, reduced to 520mm. Thirty-four locomotives were built by SLM, between 1911 and 1916, and they were Series Eb 3/5 SBB Group 52. The engines were all built with super-heaters.

No 5811 (SLM 2212/11) is preserved and is on display at Baden. This locomotive carries the works plates of SLM 1798/07, a 2–6–0T (!).

Engine No 5810 (SLM 2211/11) was sold to the Mittelthurgau Railway (M-Th-B) in 1964. It now has no number and is stored at Wil.

No 5819 (SLM 2220/12) is stored at Vallorbe and is scheduled for preservation at the *Verkehrshaus* at Lucerne.

Dimensions: CYLINDERS: 520 × 600mm
             COUPLED WHEELS: 1520mm
             GRATE AREA: 2.3m²
             BOILER PRESSURE: 12atm
             SUPERHEATED

M- Th-B 2–6–2WT No 1, identical with No 3 [Brian Stephenson

Mittelthurgau Railway (M-Th-B). Four superheated 2–6–2 Well Tank locomotives were built in 1912 by SLM, for this 42km-long railway which was opened in 1911. They were series Ec 3/5, they carried the running numbers 1–4 and were SLM 2261–4 respectively. Three were withdrawn in 1966 after completion of electrification of the line but No 3 remains in store at Wil and is used occasionally for rail tours. It will be preserved.

Dimensions: CYLINDERS: 435 × 600mm
COUPLED WHEELS: 1230mm
GRATE AREA: 1.55m²
BOILER PRESSURE: 12atm

E–B 2–8–0T No 8 Series Ed 4/5   [Fr. Neuenschwander

Emmental Railway (E-B) No 8 Series E 4/5 is one of four 2–8–0T built by SLM, the first two in 1899, the third in 1909 and the fourth, No 8, in 1914. The three older locomotives were two-cylinder compounds but No 8 (SLM 2427/14) is a two-cylinder simple with piston valves and superheated. Although electrification of this 42km-long railway was completed in 1932, No 8 is now on the Vereinigte Huttwill Railway and is kept at Eriswil. It will certainly be preserved when it is finally retired.

Dimensions: CYLINDERS: 470 × 600mm
        COUPLED WHEELS: 1230mm
        GRATE AREA: $1.7m^2$
        BOILER PRESSURE: 12atm
        SUPERHEATED

S–M–B 2–8–0 T No 11 [Fr. Neuenschwander

Solothurn-Munster Railway (S-M-B) No 11 (SLM 2160/11). A "one-off" heavy superheated tank engine of pleasing proportions built in 1911 for this 23 kilometre railway with ruling gradients of 1 in 36 (28⁰/₀₀). The line was electrified in 1932 and No 11 was kept in reserve. In 1966 it was placed on display in Oberdorf.

Dimensions: CYLINDERS: 570 × 640mm

              COUPLED WHEELS: 1330mm

              GRATE AREA: $2.2m^2$

              BOILER PRESSURE: 12atm

              SUPERHEATED

S–C–B 0–4–4–0 Mallet No 196 on display at the Verkehrshaus at Lucerne [P. R–W

Swiss Central Railway (S-C-B) No 196, SBB No 7696 (Maffei 1710/93) Type Ed 2 × 2/2 SBB Group 67, is a four-cylinder compound Mallet tank locomotive which is preserved at the *Verkehrshaus* at Lucerne.

This locomotive was withdrawn in 1938 and was stored until 1957 when it was restored for the museum.

The S-C-B had 16 four-cylinder compound Mallet tank engines built by Maffei for freight service between 1891 and 1893. Twelve larger Mallet 0–4–4–0 tender engines were built by SLM for the same railway in 1897 and 1900. All 28 Mallets came into the SBB in 1902. (In 1890, Maffei built one 0–6–6–0 Mallet tank for the Gotthard Railway but the order was not repeated.)

With the successful development of articulated locomotives of both the Mallet and Garratt types for heavily graded lines in other parts of the world it is, perhaps, surprising that the Swiss Railways never made more use of them.

Dimensions: CYLINDERS: HIGH PRESSURE: 350 × 610mm
LOW PRESSURE: 540 × 610mm
COUPLED WHEELS: 1200mm
GRATE AREA: 1.7m²
BOILER PRESSURE: 14atm

From 1886 until 1930, 39 steam railcars were built for Swiss railways. A comparatively small number, but what they lost in quantity they certainly gained in variety, for they were built for standard gauge railways, narrow gauge railways, tramways, rack and adhesion lines and pure rack (for the Pilatus Railway). Boilers were placed lengthways or across the vehicle and some had vertical boilers. Many were superheated and on the Bern and the Geneva tramways boiler pressures as high as 30atm and 20atm respectively, were used.

Despite their mechanical interest, it is probable that, apart from the 800mm-gauge Pilatus Railway vehicles, only one steam railcar will be preserved. This is the first 1435mm-gauge steam railcar to run in Switzerland and it was built at Esslingen in 1902 for the North Eastern Railway (N-O-B) as their No 1, coming under SBB ownership later that year. It is a two-axle vehicle, two outside cylinders with Walschaerts valve gear driving the leading wheels. The boiler was originally of the water tube type being the first of the Serpollet system to be built. Boiler pressure was 25atm and the system included a superheater.

In 1907 the railcar was reconstructed and a vertical Kittel type superheated boiler was substituted. At the same time the vehicle was sold to the Uerikon-Bauma Railway as their No 31. It was withdrawn in 1950 and is at present at Vallorbe awaiting preservation in the *Verkehrshaus der Schweiz* at Lucerne.

Dimensions: CYLINDERS: 220 × 300mm

COUPLED WHEELS: 1020mm BOILER PRESSURE: 16atm

GRATE AREA: 0.7m² SUPERHEATED

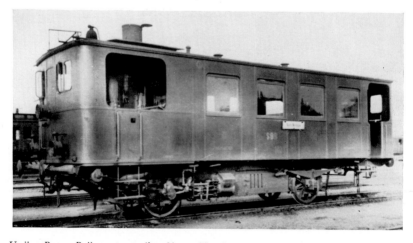

Uerikon-Bauma Railway steam railcar No 31. The photograph shows the vehicle in SBB livery soon after reconstruction [SBB

Rack Railways

The steepest gradients on a railway on which adhesion working is practicable are 1 in 15 (6.6 per cent) for short inclines where the momentum gained by the train before reaching the incline helps to carry it over the top, and in 1 in 25 (4 per cent) for longer inclines. When steeper gradients have to be climbed a rack railway may be laid.

A rack railway may be defined as one in which the tractive force of the locomotive is transmitted wholly or partly through a cogged wheel (or rack pinion—the words are used synonymously), engaging in a toothed rail or a steel ladder usually laid between the running rails.

Rack railways fall broadly into two categories depending on the length and severity of the inclines of the line.

(1) When the line has some gradients more severe than 1 in 15 but has others far less steep and may even have parts of the route which are level, then a system known as *Rack and Adhesion* is employed. The rack is laid only on the steeper gradients and the locomotives at first had one set of cylinders to drive both rack pinion and adhesion wheels. This was an unsatisfactory arrangement and was superseded by locomotives built with two separate engines supplied with steam from one boiler. Outside cylinders and motion drive coupled wheels in the normal manner and are controlled by their own regulator and reverser. Inside cylinders also with their own controls, drive a pair of cogged wheels usually through reduction gearing. The cogged wheels are synchronised by coupling rods and are supported by their own frames which are in turn fixed inside the locomotive main frames.

When working on the easier gradients and level stretches, the adhesion part of the locomotive, the outside cylinders and coupled wheels only are used. When on the severe rack gradients both the adhesion part and the rack engine are used, though each remains a separately controlled unit.

At the commencement of each rack section there is a sprung "lead-in" section to the rack rail. On rack and adhesion lines trains may be pushed or pulled by the locomotive; when they are pulled it is usual to have a banking locomotive in the rear to prevent the possibility of a break away. All the vehicles are coupled to each other and to the locomotive.

(2) A rack railway is said to be *Pure Rack* when the great majority of the gradients are too steep for adhesion working and the locomotives are propelled only by their cogged wheels or rack pinions engaging in the rack. There is no drive to the flanged carrying wheels which are used only for guiding and carrying the locomotive (but may sometimes be used for braking purposes). Pure rack is used always for mountain railways. The freight wagons or passenger coaches are always pushed by the locomotive up the incline and they are not coupled to the locomotive; gravity causes them to be kept in close contact either when ascending or descending. Should the locomotive run away or become derailed it will not drag its train with it; trains are fitted with independent emergency braking systems.

Ostermundigen-Steinbruch Railway. The first rack and adhesion locomotive in Switzerland was built in 1871 by the works of the Swiss Central Railway in Olten for the Ostermundigen-Steinbruch 1435mm-gauge railway near Bern. It was used to propel freight wagons from the S-C-B station at Ostermundigen to a factory at Sandsteinbruch, nearly $1\frac{1}{2}$km away and involving a climb of 1 in 10 ($100^0/_{00}$), using the Riggenbach rack system.

Unlike later rack and adhesion locomotives in which two cylinders drove the rack and two others the adhesion wheels, in this early engine and in those which immediately followed, two cylinders did both duties. The drive was to a layshaft on which were gear wheels which drove the rack pinion while another set of gear wheels drove cranks from which connecting rods turned the adhesion wheels.

Rack and adhesion locomotive No 1 GNOM   [SBB

No 1 *GNOM* was built in 1871 by S-C-B, Olten (works number 20). It has back tanks and an open cab. No 2 *ELFE* which followed in 1876 has side tanks, an enclosed cab and is, in appearance, completely different from its predecessor. It was built in 1876 by Gesellschaft Bergbahnen, Aarau (works number 10). No 1 is a 2–2–0T with outside cylinders and No 2 is an 0–4–0T with inside cylinders.

Rack and adhesion locomotive No 2 ELFE as von Roll No 6   [SBB

The Steinbruch Railway closed in 1902 and the two locomotives went
to the von Roll Company, No 1 to the works at Rondez where it became
No 7 and No 2 to Gerlafingen as No 6 in the von Roll list. The locomotives
were retired in 1940 and 1941 respectively and are now in store at
Vallorbe, scheduled for preservation in the *Verkehrshaus der Schweiz* at
Lucerne.

Dimensions: No 1: CYLINDERS: 270 × 400mm
DRIVING WHEELS: (adhesion) 1150mm
GRATE AREA: 0.7m^2
BOILER PRESSURE: 10atm

No 2: CYLINDERS: 300 × 500mm
DRIVING WHEELS: (adhesion) 1150mm
GRATE AREA: 1.0m^2
BOILER PRESSURE: 10atm

Vitznau-Rigi Railway (R-B). This 1435mm gauge mountain railway has a ruling gradient of 1 in 4 ($250^0/_{00}$) and is 6.9km in length. It was the first of 15 pure rack railways to be built in Switzerland and was completed in 1871. It has used electric traction since 1937.

R–B No 7 at the Verkehrshaus, Lucerne   [Verkehrshaus der Schweiz

The Riggenbach rack system is used and the railway was first operated by vertical boilered steam locomotives carried on four wheels. These locomotives were later rebuilt with horizontal locomotive type boilers and some were superheated. The first six locomotives were built between 1870 and 1872 at the works of the Swiss Central Railway at Olten. Subsequent locomotives were built by SLM and the first of these, R-B No 7 (SLM 1/73) has been restored to its original condition with a vertical boiler. It is preserved at the *Verkehrshaus* at Lucerne. The two outside cylinders which drive the rack pinions through single reduction gear wheels, have slide valves actuated by Allan straight link motion. The flanged rail wheels carry and guide the locomotive but are not driven.

Dimensions: CYLINDERS: 270 × 400mm

         GRATE AREA: 0.9m^2

         BOILER PRESSURE: 10atm

R–B No 17 Class 11/3 H at Rigi-Kulm [Brian Stephenson

No 16 and No 17 Class II '3 H are the last two steam locomotives to be built for the R-B. They are preserved in working order at Vitznau and are used from time to time to work special trains up the mountain.

Both locomotives were built by SLM, No 16 in 1923 (works number 2871) and No 17 in 1925 (works number 3043). They were both built with superheaters.

There are six flanged carrying wheels the last two of which are in a pony truck. None of the carrying wheels is driven.

Dimensions: CYLINDERS: 340 × 450mm
GRATE AREA: 0.9m²
BOILER PRESSURE: 13kg/cm²
SUPERHEATED

247

Narrow Gauge Railways of Switzerland

There is a considerable number of narrow gauge railways in Switzerland and, apart from the pure rack mountain railways which will be considered later, these railways are, with one exception, laid to a gauge of 1000mm (1.00m) and nearly all of the lines are single track many having rack and adhesion sections. The exception to the metre gauge is that of the 14km long Waldenburgerbahn which is laid to a gauge of 750mm.

Of the metre-gauge lines SBB own only the 74km of the partly rack and adhesion-operated Brünig line. The remainder of the 1624km of single track metre gauge railway is owned by no fewer than 65 private companies most of which have, for economic reasons, amalgamated into groups.

With the exception of the 4.8km of the metre-gauge Meiringen-Innertkirchen line which is diesel operated, all the narrow gauge lines are electrically operated though the electric systems employed are not all the same.

Many of the metre-gauge lines, were, at first, steam operated and subsequent electrification resulted in the scrapping, selling or preserving of the steam engines which worked them.

An interesting metre-gauge line which is, in itself, a railway museum is the 9km-long Blonay-Chamby Tourist Railway situated at an altitude of 750m to the north of Lake Leman. It is electrified but operates both electric railcars and steam locomotives. The latter form an interesting collection of engines, acquired or on loan, from several European railways. These are listed under their countries of origin.

Details of those Swiss locomotives which have been preserved are given in the following pages.

Rh-B 2–8–0 No 108   [Brian Stephenson

Rhätische Bahn (Rh-B). The Rhaetian Railway. This is by far the most complex and the longest of the Swiss metre-gauge railways having a route kilometrage of 276km.

Despite a ruling gradient of 1 in 22 $(45^0/_{00})$ the line is adhesion only and has no rack sections. The company completed electrification of the line in 1922 but has preserved several steam locomotives which are used to haul occasional special trains. Two of these locomotives are 2–8–0s Series G 4/5 with four-wheeled tenders. No 107 (SLM 1709/06) which is kept at Landquart and No 108 (SLM 1710/06) at Samedan. They are the survivors of 23 similar locomotives built by SLM between 1906 and 1915 all with superheaters and piston valves. Their immediate predecessors (1904–06) were six non-superheated two-cylinder compound 2–8–0s, the first four of which had smaller boilers than the other two.

Dimensions: CYLINDERS: 440 × 580mm
COUPLED WHEELS: 1050mm
GRATE AREA: 2.1m^2
BOILER PRESSURE: 12atm
SUPERHEATED

SWITZERLAND   1000mm
0–6–0 Tram Engines

Stadtische Strassenbahnen, Bern (S-B-B). Eight 0–6–0 Well Tank engines with enclosed wheels and motion and having Joy valve gear operated this tramway before it was electrified. The engines were numbered 11–18 and were built by SLM in 1894. Two are preserved: No 12 (works number 863) which went to Holzwerk Renfer, Biel, in 1908 is now stored in the buildings of part of the projected *Technorama* at Winterthur. (It may not remain there as *Technorama* is not to be a transport museum.)

No 18 (works number 890) was sold to the Stansstad-Engelberg Railway to become their No 15 in 1904. In 1953 it was retired and in 1958 was placed in the *Verkehrshaus* at Lucerne.

Dimensions: CYLINDERS: 240 × 350mm
  COUPLED WHEELS: 750mm
  GRATE AREA: 0.4m²
  BOILER PRESSURE: 14atm

Stadtische Strassenbahnen, Bern (SSB) No 13 (SLM 864/94) which was No 3 of the Bern-Worbbahn from 1903 to 1913. This is a sister locomotive to No 12 [Technorama Winterthur

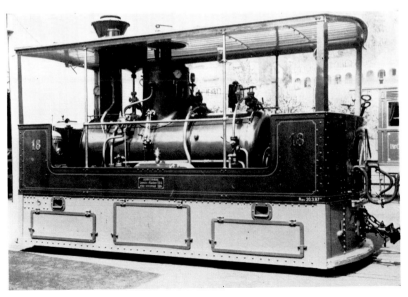

Stansstad-Engelberg No 18 [Verkehrshaus der Schweiz

SWITZERLAND   0–6–0T   1000mm

Frauenfeld-Wil Railway (F-W). Engine No 2 (SLM 462/87) is an 0–6–0T with Brown valve gear. The coupled wheels are inside the frames, the cranks, motion and cylinders are outside the frames. The slide valves are placed below the cylinders.

No 2 carries the name plates *HÖRNLI* from engine No 4 of the same class. It was withdrawn in 1921 and was stored by the railway. It has recently been restored by the *Modelleisenbahnklub* and will be placed on display at Wil.

Dimensions: CYLINDERS: 240 × 350mm
                 COUPLED WHEELS: 750mm
                 GRATE AREA: 0.5m²
                 BOILER PRESSURE: 14atm

Regional des Brenets (R-d-B) is a short line, only 4km in length operating between le Locle and les Brenets on the French frontier in the Jura. It has been electrified since 1950 before which date it was operated by three little 0–6–0 tank engines Nos 1, 2, 3 (SLM 618 and 619 of 1890 and 716/92). The design was very compact, the six coupled wheels being inside the frames with the cranks, motion and cylinders outside. Walschaerts valve gear operated slide valves above the cylinders.

No 1 *LE DOUBS* is now stored at Vallorbe and is reserved for the *Verkehrshaus der Schweiz*.

No 3 LES BRENETS

[Fr. Neuenschwander

No 2 *LE PERE FREDERIC* is stored in the ownership of the railway.

No 3 *LES BRENETS* has been sectioned and part is now used for instruction in the Technical School at le Locle.

Dimensions: CYLINDERS: 240 × 380mm
           COUPLED WHEELS: 750mm
           GRATE AREA: 0.4m^2
           BOILER PRESSURE: 12atm

SBB No 109, ex Jura-Simplon Railway No 909 (SLM 1341/01) Series G 3/3. Worked on the Brünig line until 1921 when it went to the 30km long Bière Apples Morges Railway (B-A-M) as their No 6 and later to Holzwerk Renfer Biel with the same number. It is a short-wheelbase outside cylinder o-6-oT with Walschaerts valve gear and slide valves on top of the cylinders. It is at present on loan to the Blonay-Chamby Tourist Railway and is being reconstructed.

Dimensions: CYLINDERS: 310 × 480mm
           COUPLED WHEELS: 1050mm
           GRATE AREA: 0.8m^2
           BOILER PRESSURE: 11atm

L–E–B No 5 formerly named BERCHER. At Feldkirch [P. R-W

Lausanne Echelons Bercher Railway (L-E-B) No 5 *BERCHER* is an out-side-cylinder 0–6–0 Side Tank locomotive which was built in 1890 by Grafenstaden (works number 4172). It is now on display at Feldkirch, Austria, in a children's playground in the Wichnergasse.

This little engine had a polished brass dome now painted over, sur-mounted by Salter safety valves. It has outside Stephenson link motion operating slide valves.

Dimensions: CYLINDERS: 270 × 370mm
           COUPLED WHEELS: 810mm
           GRATE AREA: 0.6m^2
           BOILER PRESSURE: 12kg/cm^2

Rh–B 2–6–0T No 11   [R. G. Farr

Rhätische Bahn (Rh-B). The Rhaetian Railway. Sixteen 2–6–0T were built by SLM between 1889 and 1908 and they worked on the Landquart-Davos section of the line. Walschaerts valve gear operated slide valves above the cylinders and the safety valves were on the dome. No 1 was built in 1889 (works number 577) for the Landquart-Davos Railway (L-D) and became Rh-B No 1 in 1895 when the L-D was taken over. It carries the name *RHÄTIA* and is at present stored at Vallorbe. In future, it may go to the Blonay-Chamby Railway. Engines No 11 (SLM 1476/02) and No 14 (SLM 1479/02) remain with the Rh-B and are used at times for special trains. No 11 is at Landquart and No 14 is at Samedan. They are Series G 3/4.

Dimensions: CYLINDERS: 340 × 500mm
            COUPLED WHEELS: 1050mm
            GRATE AREA: 0.9m² for No 1
                      1.0m² for Nos 11 and 14
            BOILER PRESSURE: 12atm

Brünig 2–6–0T No 208 (adhesion only) [SBB

SBB No 208 (SLM 2403/13) was one of eight 2–6–0T Series G 3/4 Group 91 built for the Brünig line by SLM between the years 1905 and 1913. The first seven engines were built without superheaters but received them from 1925 to 1927. No 208, however, was superheated when built but, like the rest of the group, had slide valves. These engines were designed for adhesion. They were all side tanks. No 208 is now privately preserved and is located at Meiringen.

Dimensions: CYLINDERS: 340 × 500mm
COUPLED WHEELS: 1050mm
GRATE AREA: 1.1m²
BOILER PRESSURE: 12atm
SUPERHEATED

W–B No 6 WALDENBURG [R. G. Farr

Waldenburg Railway (W-B). During the 30 years 1882–1912, this 14km-long railway had five 0–6–0T the first of which was built by Krauss and the others by SLM. In the earlier engines, the coupled wheels were inside the frames and the cranks, motion and cylinders were outside. The second No 4 and Nos 5 and 6 had the normal arrangement of wheels, cylinders and motion outside the frames. They were Series G 3/3 and they were the smallest locomotives in Switzerland.

No 5 *G. THOMMEN* (SLM 1440/02) was withdrawn in 1954 when the railway was electrified and is now on display at Liestal.

No 6 *WALDENBURG* (SLM 2276/12) was withdrawn in 1954 and preserved by the *Amateurklub*, Lucerne. In 1958 it was installed in the *Verkehrshaus der Schweiz*.

Dimensions: CYLINDERS: 260 × 350mm
COUPLED WHEELS: 750mm
GRATE AREA: 0.5m^2
BOILER PRESSURE: 14atm

F–O Rack and adhesion 2–6–0 T No 3   [Brian Stephenson

Furka-Oberalp Railway (F-O). This is one of the more recent narrow gauge railways having been completed as late as 1915. It was known originally as the Brig-Furka-Disentis Railway and the first 46km were opened to traffic in June 1914. It is the second longest metre-gauge line in Switzerland, its 100.2 route kilometres being exceeded only by the 276km of the *Rhätische Bahn*.

The line runs from Disentis to Brig, crossing over the top of the Gotthard Tunnel near Andermatt.

With a ruling gradient of 1 in 9.1 ($110^0/_{00}$) it was necessary for part of the line, 32km in all, to be rack operated and, for this purpose, the Abt system was chosen.

To work the line, in 1913–14, SLM supplied ten four-cylinder compound 2–6–0 superheated tank locomotives. The high pressure cylinders are outside and drive the adhesion wheels in the usual manner. The two low pressure cylinders are inside and drive two coupled axles supported by their own frames inside the main engine frames. The rack pinions are driven by these axles. The need to locate the large LP cylinders inside, necessitated the main frames being more widely spaced and, as a result, the adhesion wheels are inside them and are driven by outside cranks. On the adhesion sections of the line, the locomotives are worked as two-cylinder simples and the compound cylinders are isolated. On the rack sections the locomotive works as a four-cylinder compound.

Only one of these locomotives now survives, this is No 4 built in 1913 by SLM (works number 2318), which is kept at Brig and occasionally works special trains.

Dimensions: CYLINDERS: HIGH PRESSURE: 420 × 480mm

LOW PRESSURE: 560 × 450mm

COUPLED WHEELS: 910mm

GRATE AREA: 1.4m^2

BOILER PRESSURE: 14atm

SBB (Brünig line) No 1063 sectioned and exhibited in the Verkehrshaus at Lucerne

[Verkehrshaus der Schweiz

SBB (Brünig line) No 1067

[R. G. Farr

SBB Brünig Line. This attractive line which runs from Lucerne to Meiringen and Interlaken, has a route length of 74km. The rack sections, which are operated on the Riggenbach System, have a ruling gradient of 1 in 8.3 ($120^0/_{00}$) while on the adhesion sections it is 1 in 40 ($25^0/_{00}$). The Brünig is the only narrow gauge line owned by SBB.

Between 1905 and 1926, SLM built 18 0–6–0 rack and adhesion tank locomotives for the line, all to the same design. They were numbered 1051–1068 and were Series $\frac{3/3}{1}$, Group 94. They had four high pressure cylinders, all outside the frames; the two which drove the rack pinions through a lay-shaft and reduction gearing were situated above the two which drove the adhesion wheels through the usual system of side rods. Each cylinder had its own slide valve operated by individual Walschaerts gear, though the die-blocks on each side of the locomotive were connected.

Three of these locomotives are preserved:

No 1063 (SLM 1993/09) with the boiler from No 1062, has been beautifully sectioned and is in the *Verkehrshaus* at Lucerne.

No 1067 (SLM 2083/10) is privately owned and is kept at Meiringen.

No 1068 (SLM 3134/26) with the boiler from No 1060 is on display at Meiringen.

Dimensions: CYLINDERS (4): 380 × 450mm
   COUPLED WHEELS: 910mm
   GRATE AREA: 1.3m^2
   WORKING PRESSURE: 14atm

Visp-Zermatt Railway (V-Z). The rack sections of this 44km-long 1000mm-gauge railway operate on the Abt system and negotiate gradients of 1 in 8 ($125^0/_{00}$). The line was electrified in 1929.

Eight 0–4–2 tank locomotives (Nos 1–8) were built for rack and adhesion working by SLM between 1890 and 1908. There were minor differences between the first six locomotives and the last two. All the locomotives carried names. They were four-cylinder simple machines, the inside cylinders driving the Abt coupled rack pinions and the outside cylinders the adhesion wheels. The valve gear was Belpaire's modification of Walschaerts. The locomotives were capable of working 45 tonnes on the 1 in 8 rack sections at 10km/h and the same train at 25km/h on the 1 in 40 gradients of the adhesion sections of the line.

No 6 *WEISSHORN* was built in 1902 by SLM (works number 1410), was sold in 1941 to the firm of Hovag at Ems and, in 1965, it was placed on display on a plinth in the Ringstrasse at Chur as part of the 500 year Trades Guild celebrations. As preserved it has had the inside rack engine removed.

No 7 *BREITHORN* was built in 1906 by SLM (works number 1725) is still owned by V-Z for special trains and is kept at Zermatt.

Dimensions: CYLINDERS (ADHESION): 360 × 450mm
(RACK): 320 × 450mm
COUPLED WHEELS: 900mm
BOILER PRESSURE: 12kg/cm²

V–Z 0–4–2T No 6 WEISSHORN on display at Chur [Brian Stephenson

V–Z 0–4–2T No 7 BREITHORN [Brian Stephenson

F–M–G No 2 preserved at Capolago   [F–M–G

Monte Generoso Railway (F-M-G). This railway which is near
Lugano, is 9km in length, has a ruling gradient of 1 in 4.5 (220⁰/₀₀) and
was opened to traffic in 1890. It is laid to a gauge of 800mm and operates
on the Abt system. Since 1954 it has been worked by diesel rack railcars
with trailers. Before that date the motive power consisted of nine steam
rack locomotives, six built for the F-M-G in 1889–90 and three bought
from the Glion-Rocher de Naye Railway (G-N) at intervals between
1941 and 1949. A further locomotive was purchased from G-N in 1956
and, with the boiler from F-M-G No 7, became Brienz-Rothorn No 1
in 1962.

All these locomotives are of the well-known SLM rack locomotive
design with two cylinders, one on each side of the boiler and situated
above the running plate. The drive from the pistons is forward to the
upper extremity of a rocking lever which, from its lower extremity, has a
connecting rod which actuates two fly cranks. These are connected
together by side rods and drive the two leading axles of the locomotive.
Keyed to the axles and between the frames are the two rack pinions.
The two leading pairs of carrying wheels are supported by the driving
axles but are not fixed to them and are not, therefore, driving wheels.
Their only functions are to guide and to support the locomotive on the
track.

One of the original F-M-G locomotives, No 2 (SLM 604/90) is now preserved at Capolago where the railway has its headquarters.

Dimensions: CYLINDERS: 300 × 550mm

GRATE AREA: 0.6m²

BOILER PRESSURE: 12atm

P–B steam railcar No 9 on a special working in 1967. Note outside flanges to carrying wheels
[Brian Stephenson

Pilatus Railway (P-B). This, the steepest of all the world's rack railways, has a ruling gradient of 1 in 2.08 (480°/₀₀) and the Riggenbach, Abt and Strub rack systems were impracticable. The Locher system was adopted with a rail gauge of 800mm and this has proved both safe and

265

P–B No 10. This photograph is of a model in the Verkehrshaus and clearly shows the design of the railcar [Verkehrshaus der Schweiz

practical. In this system the toothed rack rail is laid on its side with the teeth facing horizontally outwards on both sides. The rack pinions which provide the sole means of traction, are keyed to vertical driving shafts on the railcars. (The railway has never owned locomotives.)

The railway was electrified in 1937. Before this it was operated by 11 steam railcars having their boilers placed athwart the engine ends of the cars. (This arrangement got over the problem of keeping the crown plates covered on such a steep gradient.) Some of the boilers were renewed at various times and some had superheaters.

Two of these interesting steam railcars, No 9 built in 1889 by SLM (works number 563) and No 10 built in 1900 by SLM (works number 1309) carry, in error, the works plates of SLM number 514 of 1888 and number 562 of 1889, respectively. Both are kept at Alpnachstad and from time to time, work special trips up the mountain.

The body of another railcar, No H I (SLM 451/86) is at Vallorbe, scheduled for preservation at the *Verkehrshaus* at Lucerne. The engine is, however, still at Alpnachstad. This railcar was reboiled and superheated in 1910, and was withdrawn in 1936.

Dimensions: CYLINDERS: 220 × 300mm

GRATE AREA: 0.4m²

BOILER PRESSURE: 12atm

Appendix 1
Locomotive Manufacturers

Abbreviated Name	Full Name

Aarau = Maschinenfabrik der Internationalen Gesellschaft fur Berg-bahnen, Aarau, Switzerland.

AB Atlas = AB Atlas, Stockholm, Sweden.

AEG = Allgemeine Elektricitats-Gesellschaft, Berlin-Grünewald.

Alco = American Locomotive Company, Schenectady, NY, USA.

Ansaldo = Società-Ansaldo-Armstrong, Sampierdarena-Genova, Italy.

Ateliers d'Oullins = PLM Company's Works at Oullins, France.

Avonside = Avonside Engine Company, Bristol, England.

Babcock & Wilcox = Sociedad Española de Constructiones Babcock & Wilcox, Sestro-Bilbao, Spain.

Baldwin = Baldwin Locomotive Company, Philadelphia, Penna, USA.

Batignolles-Châtillon = Batignolles-Châtillon Paris and Nantes, France.

Berlin = Berliner Maschinenbau AG, Vormals L. Schwartzkopff, Berlin.

B.P. = Beyer Peacock & Co, Gorton, Manchester, England.

Blanc-Misseron = (ANF) Ateliers de Constructions du Nord de la France, Crespin-Blanc-Misseron (Nord), les Mureaux.

Borsig = A. Borsig, Berlin-Tegel, Germany.

Boussu = S.A. des Ateliers de Construction du Boussu, Boussu, Belgium.

Breda (Italy) = Ernesto Breda, Milan, Italy.

Breda (Netherlands) = Machinefabriek Backer & Rueb, Breda, Holland.

Buddicom = Allcard Buddicom, Chartreux, Rouen, France.

Cail = J. F. Cail = Société Française de Constructions Mecaniques, Denain, France.

Canada Works = Peto, Betts & Brassey, Canada Works, Birkenhead, England.

Canadian = Canadian Locomotive Works, Montreal, Canada.

Chaplin = Alex. Chaplin & Co, Cranston Hill Engine Works, Glasgow.

Chemnitz = Sachsische Maschinenfabrik, vormals Richard Hartmann, Chemnitz, Germany.

Cockerill = John Cockerill, Seraing, Belgium.

Corpet Louvet = Société Corpet Louvet et Cie, La Courneuve, France.

Couillet = Société Anonyme des Usines Metallurgiques du Hainaut, Couillet, Marcinelle, Belgium.

Decauville = Société Anonyme Decauville, Corbeil, France.

Dübs = Dübs & Co., Scotland.

Erste Böhmische-Marische Maschinenfabrik = First Bohemian-Moravian Engine Works, Prague, Czechoslovakia.

Esslingen = Maschinenfabrik Esslingen-Mettingen, Esslingen am Neckar, Germany.

Est = Est Railway Works, Epernay, France.

Euskalduna = Compañia Euskalduna de Construction y Reparacion de Buques SA, Bilbao, Spain.

Fairbairn = W. Fairbairn & Sons, Canal Street Works, Manchester, England.

Falun = Vagn & Maskinfabriks AB, Falun, Sweden.

Abbreviated Name	Full Name

F.A.M.H. = Compagnie des Forges et Aciéries de la Marine d'Homé-court, France.

Fives = Compagnie de Fives-Lille pour Constructions Mecaniques et Enterprises, Fives-Lille, France.

Fletcher Jennings = Fletcher Jennings & Company, Lowca Works, Whitehaven, England.

Floridsdorf = Wiener Lokomotivfabrik, AG, Wien-Floridsdorf, Austria.

Fox Walker = Fox, Walker & Co., Bristol, England.

Franco-Belge = Société Franco-Belge de Matériel de Chemins de Fer, La Croyère, Belgium.

Freudenstein = Freudenstein AG, Berlin, Germany.

Frichs = A/S Frichs, Maskinfabrik, Aarhus, Denmark.

Gouin = Ernst Gouin, Etablissement Gouin, Paris, France.

Graffenstaden = Société Usine de Graffenstaden, Graffenstaden, France.

Hagans = Christian Hagans, Erfurt, Germany.

Haine-St. Pierre = Société Anonyme des Forges, Usines et Fonderies, Haine-St. Pierre, Belgium.

Hallette = Alfred Hallette, Arras, France.

Hamar = Jernstöper & Maskinfabrik, Hamar, Norway.

Hanomag = Hannoversche Maschinenbau AG vormals Georg Egestorff, Hannover-Linden, Germany.

Hartmann = Maschinenfabrik Richard Hartmann, Chemnitz, Germany.

Haswell = John Haswell Lokomotivfabrik (later StEG), Wien, Austria.

Heilbronn = Maschinenfabrik, Heilbronn, Germany.

Henschel = Henschel & Söhn, Cassel (later, Henschel-Werke GmbH, Kassel, Germany).

Helsingfors = Railway Works, Helsinki, Finland.

Hohenzollern = Hohenzollern AG fur Lokomotivbau, Dusseldorf-Grafenberg, Germany.

Hudswell Clark = Hudswell Clark & Company, Railway Foundry, Leeds, England.

Henry Hughes = Henry Hughes, Falcon Works, Loughborough, England.

Humboldt = Humboldt Lokomotivbau, Köln-Kalk, Germany.

Hunslet = The Hunslet Engine Works, Leeds, England.

Jones & Potts = Jones & Potts, Newton-le-Willows, Lancs., England.

Jones = Jones, Turner & Evans, Warrington, England.

Jung = Arn. Jung Lokomotivfabrik GmbH, Jungenthal bei Kirchberg, Germany.

Kalmar = Kalmar Verkstads AB, Kalmar, Sweden.

Karlsruhe = See Kessler.

Kessler = Maschinenfabrik von Emil Kessler, Karlsruhe, Germany.

Koechlin = Lokomotivfabrik André Koechlin & Cie, Mulhouse, France.

Krauss = Lokomotivfabrik Krauss & Co., München, Germany.

Krauss-Linz = Lokomotivfabrik Krauss & Co., Linz an der Donau, Austria.

Krauss-Maffei = Krauss-Maffei AG, München-Allach, Germany.

Kristinehamn = Kristinehamns Mekaniska Verkstad, Kristinehamn, Sweden.

Krupp = Fried. Krupp, Maschinenfabriken, Essen, Germany.

Abbreviated Name	Full Name

Lima = Lima Locomotive Company, Lima, Ohio, USA.
Linke-Hofmann = Linke-Hofmann Werke, Breslau, Germany.
Lokomo = Lokomo Oy, Tampere, Finland.
Longridge = R. B. Longridge & Co., Bedlington Iron Works, Northumberland, England.
Macosa = Material y Construcciones SA, Valencia, Spain.
Maffei = J. A. Maffei AG, München, Germany.
Manning Wardle = Manning Wardle & Co. Ltd., Boyne Engine Works, Leeds, England.
Maquinista = La Maquinista Terrestre y Maritima, Barcelona, Spain.
Merryweather = Merryweather & Sons, Greenwich, England.
La Meuse = S.A. des Ateliers de Construction de la Meuse, Sclessin-Liège, Belgium.
Montreal = Montreal Locomotive Works, Montreal, Canada.
Motala = Motala Mekaniska Verkstad, Motala, Sweden.
Munktells = Th. Munktells, Mekaniska Verkstad, Eskilstuna, Sweden.
Neilson = Neilson & Co., Glasgow, Scotland.
NOHAB = Nydquist & Holm AB, Trollhättan, Sweden.
Nord = Chemin de Fer du Nord Railway Works, La Chapelle, Paris, France.
Norris = Norris Works at Wien (affiliated to Norris Locomotive Works, Philadelphia, USA).
NBL = North British Locomotive Company, Glasgow, Scotland.
Nydquist = Nydquist & Holm (see NOHAB, above).
Olten = Swiss Central Railway Works at Olten, Switzerland.
OM = Officine Meccaniche, Milan, Italy.
Oullins = Parent & Schaken, Oullins, France.
Orenstein = Orenstein & Koppel, Berlin-Drewitz, Germany.
Parent = Société Parent, Schaken, Caillet et Cie, Fives, Lille, France.
PLM = Works of the P.L.M. at Arles, France.
Postula = Postula & Cie, Renaud Works, Brussels, Belgium.
Richmond = Richmond Locomotive Works, Richmond, Va., USA.
Saronno = Costruzioni Meccaniche Saronno, Italy.
Sentinel = Sentinel Wagon Works Ltd., Shrewsbury, England.
Schneider = Schneider & Cie, Le Creusot, France.
Schwartzkopff = L. Schwartzkopff AG, Berlin, Germany.
Sharp Stewart = Sharp Stewart & Co., Ltd., Glasgow, Scotland.
Skoda = Skoda-Werke, Filsen, Czechoslovakia.
Slaughter-Grüning = Slaughter-Grüning & Co., Fishponds, Bristol, England.
SLM = Swiss Locomotive and Machine Company, Winterthur, Switzerland.
Société Alsacienne = SACM = Société Alsacienne de Constructions Mécaniques, Graffenstaden, Mulhouse, France.
St. Leonard = Société Anonyme des Ateliers, St. Leonard, Liege, Belgium.
Robert Stephenson = Robert Stephenson & Co., Newcastle-upon-Tyne, England.
StEG = Wien-Gloggnitz Railway Works, Wien, Austria (later became

Maschinenfabrik der k.k.priv. österreichischen staats-eisenbahnen Gesellschaft, Wien).

Tampereen = Tampereen Pellava Oy, Tampere, Finland.

Tayleur = Charles Tayleur & Co., Newton-le-Willows, Lancs., England.

Thunes = Thunes Mekaniske Verkstad, Oslo, Norway.

Tubize = Société Générale d'Exploitation, Morel-Zaman, Tubize, Belgium.

Turin = FS Railway Works, Turin, Italy.

Vulcan = A/S Vulcan Works, Maribo, Denmark.

Werkspoor = Nederlandsche Fabrik van Werktuigen en Spoorwegmaterieel, Amsterdam, Holland.

Wiener-Neustadt = Lokomotivfabrik, vormals G. Sigl, Wiener-Neustadt, Austria.

Yorkshire = Yorkshire Engine Company Ltd., Sheffield, England.

Zobel = Locomotivfabrik L. Zobel, Bromberg, Germany.

Appendix 2

Location of Preserved and Stored Locomotives

Italy

Location	Number	Type
Brescia, Castle Park	1 SNFT	0-6-0T
Laona, Park	9 *SATTI*	0-6-0T
Marina di Pietrasanta	895.028	0-8-0T
Milan, Leonardo da Vinci Museum	*Bayard* (REP)	2-2-2
	552.036	4-4-0
	s685.600	2-6-2
	691.022	4-6-2
	746.031	2-8-2
	470.092	0-10-0
	BG 34 *Trezzo*	0-4-0T Tram
	III	0-4-0T Tram
	835.186	0-6-0T
	250.05	0-6-0T
	880.159	2-6-0T
	940.001	2-8-2T
Rome, Smistamento Depot FS	290.319	0-6-0*
	640.106	2-6-0*
	680.037	2-6-2*
	736.202	2-8-0*
	22	4-4-0T*
	830.035	0-6-0T*
	905.032	2-6-0T*
	910.001	2-6-2T*
	980.002	0-6-0RT*
Turin, Smistamento Depot FS	800.008	0-4-0T*
Turin, Private estate	6801 *Garigliante*	0-6-0T

Italy—Narrow Gauge

Location	Number	Type
Rome, Smistamento Depot FS	R410.004	0-8-0WT
	302.23	2-6-0T
Milan, Leonardo da Vinci Museum	P 7	0-8-2T
	301.2	2-6-0T

Netherlands

Location	Number	Type
Bergen, on display in village	7742	0-6-0T
Breda, in garden of N.V. Machine-fabrik	22 GST	0-4-0T Tram

* *The locomotive is stored and, therefore, the location given is not permanent.*
(REP) = Replica.

Location	Number	Type
Enschede, Stichting Museum	8107	0–4–0T
Hoorn	18 GST	0–4–0T Tram
	Leeghwater	
Utrecht, Railway Museum	2 *De Arend* (REP)	2–2–2
	13	2–4–0
	89 *Nestor*	2–4–0
	326	2–4–0
	107	4–4–0
	2104	4–4–0
	3737	4–6–0
	73755	2–10–0
	6317	4–8–4T
	2 RSTM	0–4–0T Tram

Netherlands—Narrow Gauge

Tramway Society, Hellevoetsluis	50 RTM	0–6–0 Tram
	54 RTM	0–6–0 Tram
	56 RTM	0–6–0 Tram
Railway Museum, Utrecht	57 RTM	0–6–0 Tram
	607 ZE	0–4–0 Tram

Norway

Bressingham Museum, Diss, England	377 *Haakon VII*	2–6–0
Hamar Railway Museum	16	2–4–0
	17	2–4–0
	470	2–8–4
	25	0–4–0T
Norwegian Railway Club	424	0–6–0T*
	288	2–6–2T*
In store for preservation, location not verified	207	2–6–0*
	255	4–6–0*
	234	4–6–0*
	271	4–6–0*
	452	4–8–0*
	11	0–4–0T*
	227	0–6–0T*

Norway—Narrow Gauge

Grovane	1	2–6–2T
	2	2–6–2T
	5	2–6–2T
	6	2–4–2T
Hamar Railway Museum	7	4–4–0
	1 *Loke*	0–4–0T
	81	2–6–4BT
	UHR 2 *Urskog*	0–6–0T
	UHR 7 *Prydz*	2–6–2T
	HGR 21 *Alf*	2–4–0T

* *The locomotive is stored and, therefore, the location given is not permanent.*
(REP)=Replica.

Location	Number	Type
Sørumsand	UHR 4 *Setskogen*	2–6–2T
	UHR 6 *Holand*	2–6–2T
Trondheim Technical School	UHR 5	
	Bjorkelangen	2–6–2T

Portugal

Abrantes Depot, CP	001	0–4–0T*
	005	0–4–0T*
Braga Depot, CP	9	2–4–0*
	02049	2–2–2T*
Estremoz Depot, CP	01 *D. Luiz*	2–2–2*
Oporto—Contumil Depot, CP	003	0–4–0T*
Vila Nova de Gaia Depot, CP	002	0–4–0T*

Spain

Alcañiz, Depot RENFE	120.2131	2–4–0*
Alcazar-de-San-Juan, Public Garden	030.2216	0–6–0
Alicante, Termino Depot, RENFE	220.2023	4–4–0*
Aguilas, Depot RENFE	130.2121 *Aguilas*	2–6–0*
	020.0231	0–4–0T*
Aravaca, Private Garden	030.0206 *El Selmo*	0–6–0T
	030.0207 *El Burbia*	0–6–0T
Barcelona, Clot Depot, RENFE	220.2005	4–4–0*
(*Museum Talleres Generals de*	030.2013	0–6–0*
Clot)	230.4001	4–6–0*
	120.2112	2–4–0T*
	030.0204 *Tarraco*	0–6–0T*
	030.0233 *Caldas*	0–6–0T*
	240.2135	4–8–0*
Bilbao, S.A. Basconia	11 *Basconia*	4–4–0T*
Calatayud, Depot RENFE	151.3101	2–10–2*
Cuenca, Depot RENFE	*Mataro* (REP)	2–2–2*
	030.2264	0–6–0*
	030.2107	0–6–0*
	040.2091 *El Cinca*	0–8–0*
	240.4001	4–8–0*
	241.2001	4–8–2*
	120.0201	2–4–0T*
Granada, In Station Square	020.0241	0–4–0T
Leon, Depot RENFE	241.4001	4–8–2*
Logroño, Sub-Depot, RENFE	230.2059	4–6–0*
	040.2082	0–8–0*
	130.0201 *Pucheta*	2–6–0T*
Lorca, Depot RENFE	030.2369	0–6–0*
Madrid, Delicias Depot, RENFE	3	2–2–2T*
Madrid Railway Museum, RENFE	020.0201	0–4–0T

* *The locomotive is stored and, therefore, the location given is not permanent.*
(REP) = Replica.

Location	Number	Type
Ponferrada, Depot RENFE	240.3001	4–8–0*
Seville, San Jeronimo Depot,	240.2081	4–8–0*
RENFE	040.2273	0–8–0*
	141.2001	2–8–2*
	9091 Sentinel Railcar*	
Tarassa, Avenida del Caudillo	020.0234	0–4–0T
Utrera, Depot RENFE	030.0202 *Jimena*	0–6–0T*
Valencia, Alameda Depot, RENFE	030.2230	0–6–0*
	030.2471	0–6–0*
	230.2085	4–6–0*
	462.F.0401 4–6–2 + 2–6–4*	
Termino Depot, RENFE	060.4013	0–6–6–0*
	020.0261	0–4–0T*
Vallodolid, Workshops, RENFE	020.0221 *Galindo*	0–4–0T*
Vigo, Depot, RENFE	030.0201	0–6–0T*
Villanueva, Depot, RENFE	030.2110 *Perruca*	0–6–0*

Spain—Narrow Gauge

Location	Number	Type
Bilbao, Basurto Station	VNR 6	0–6–0T
Castellon Station	OGCR I	0–6–0T
Durango	VR 104 *Aurrera*	2–6–0T
Guernica	AGBR I	
	Zugastieta	0–6–0T
Martorell Empalme	CGFC 33	0–6–0T
Sagunto Steel Works	VR 103 *Orcanera*	0–6–0T
Tortosa Park	VR Tortosa la	
	Cava 1	4–4–0T
Vallodolid Park	CSR 2 *Rioseca*	0–4–0T

Sweden

Location	Number	Type
Älmhult, Depot, SJ	1814	4–4–0*
Almhult station	SOEJ 1	2–4–0T
Avesta Jernverk	KNJ 2 *Bjurfors*	2–6–0T
Borås, *Nybroparken*	1551	0–6–0*
Borås, in service	576	0–8–0T
Eskilstuna, Museum TGOJ	OFWJ 1	0–6–0T*
Gävle, Railway Museum	75 *Göta*	2–2–2
(provisional list of exhibits)	3 *Prins August*	2–4–0
	347	2–4–0
	198 *Breda*	2–4–0
	OFWJ 8	0–4–2
	404	4–4–0
	1001	4–4–2
	93 *Jernsida*	0–6–0
	BJ 27	0–6–0
	390	0–6–0
	864	4–6–0
	779	2–8–0

The locomotive is stored and, therefore, the location given is not permanent.

Location	Number	Type
Gävle, Railway Museum (cont.)	UWHJ 1	
	Trollhättan	2–4–oT
	22 *Thor*	o–4–2T
	FKAJ *Frykstad*	o–6–oT
Hultsfred Hembygdsparken	1774	4–4–o
Kristianstad, Museum	OSJ 15	2–6–o
	1655	2–6–o
Karlskoga, outside Station NKJ	NKJ 1 *Karlskoga*	o–6–oT
Linköping, Museum	692	o–6–o
Nässjö, Stadsparken	MASJ 3 *Tyr*	o–6–oT*
Narvik, Norway. Depot NSB	HHyJ 5	4–4–oT*
Östersund, Depot SJ	1200	4–6–2*
Trelleborg, Museum	LLTJ 15	2–4–4T
	2 *Malmköping*	2–6–oT
Västerås, Depot SJ	1714	2–6–o
Location unknown (in reserve)	1026	4–6–o*
	900	o–8–o*

Sweden—Narrow Gauge
600mm Gauge

Location	Number	Type
	SJ (BYCF) 10	o–4–oT
Railway Museum, Gävle	KLJ 2 *Kessebo*	o–4–4–oT
Östra Sodermanlands Järnväg	SJ (BYCF) 1 *Lotta*	o–4–oT
	3 *Dylta*	o–4–oT
	6 *Smedjebacken*	o–4–oT
	7 *Helgenas*	o–4–2T
	StJ 2 *Vira*	2–4–2T
	4 *K.M. Nelsson*	2–6–2T
	5 *Hamra*	o–4–4–oT
	8 *Emsfors*	o–8–oT
Skärstad Museum	JGJ 19	2–6–2T

802mm Gauge

Location	Number	Type
Gävle, Railway Museum	SVJ 4 *Sebastian Grave*	o–6–4T
Hälsingborg, Friluftmuseum	HFJ 7	2–8–2T
Nora Station	WMJ 4	2–6–oT

891mm Gauge

Location	Number	Type
Borgholm, Gamla Bangården	SOJ 6	2–8–oT
Gävle, Railway Museum	SRJ 28	2–6–2
	DONJ 12	o–6–6–o
	SRJ 3 *Runbo*	2–4–oT
	GJ 3 *Gotland*	2–4–oT
Hagfors Station	NKlJ 1 UA	o–4–2T
	NKlJ 5	o–6–oT
Jadraas Museisallskap	MKlJ 9	2–4–oT
	VAHJ 2	o–6–2T
Hjo, Gamla Bangården	VGJ 4	2–6–oT
Kalmar Park	SJ 3037	2–6–2T
Långshyttan, Bangårder	BLJ 5 *Thor*	2–8–o
	BLJ 2 *Kloster*	o–6–oT

* *The locomotive is stored and, therefore, the location given is not permanent.*

Location	Number	Type
891mm Gauge (continued)		
Linköping Museum	NOJ 18	2–8–2T
Målilla	KlRJ 1	0–6–0T
Nassjo, Hembygdsparken	HvSJ 4	0–6–0T
Roma, Gamla Bangården	SlRJ	2–8–0T
Skara, Bangården	VGJ 29	2–8–0
Stockholm Roslagens Museiforening	SJ 3132	2–8–0
Stora Lundby Museum Railway	VGJ 31	4–6–0
	VGJ 24	4–6–0
	Gota I	0–4–0T
	KBJ 5 *Nanna*	4–4–0T
	ROJ 3	2–6–0T
	BLJ 6	2–8–0T
Vastervik Station	HVJ 22	2–6–0
Västra Frölunda Lekplats	NKlJ 24	2–8–0T
Yxhults S'hugger	UJ 1	0–6–0T
1067mm Gauge		
Kristianstad Museum	WBlJ 19	4–4–0T
Upsala Depot, SJ	BKB 9	2–6–0*
1093mm Gauge		
Köping Museum	KUJ 7 *Patric Reutersward*	0–6–0T

Switzerland

Location	Number		Type	
Adliswil, *Schule Werd*	4	SihlTB	0–6–0T	
Attisholz, in service	3	GTB	0–6–0T	
Baden, station, SBB	5811	SBB	2–6–2T	
Basle, Gasworks	2	SihlTB	0–6–0T	
Bern, Schwarzenac	51	BSB	2–6–0T	
Buchs, Station SBB	8487	SBB	0–6–0T	
Degersheim, on display	6	BT	2–6–2T	
Dornach, Metalwerke	72	TSB	0–4–0T*	
Einsiedeln, on display	4	SOB *Schwyz*	0–6–0T	
Emmenbrucke, in service	41	SCB	0–6–0T	
Eriswil	8	EB	2–8–0T*	
Erstfeld, station	2965	SBB	2–10–0	
Herisau, *Dampflok-Klub*	9	BT	2–6–2T	
Horgen, *Schule Tannenbach*	3	SihlTB	0–6–0T	
Kleinhuningen, Children's Playground	453	NOB	0–6–0T	
Lucerne, *Verkehrshaus der Schweiz*	1	NOB *Limmat*	4–2–0	(REP)
	11	GB	0–4–0T	
	28	SCB *Genf*	0–4–6T	
	196	SCB	0–4–4–0T	

* *The locomotive is stored and, therefore, the location given is not permanent.*
(REP) = Replica.

Location	Number	Type
Lucerne, *Verkehrshaus der Schweiz*	2978 SBB	2–10–0
	7 RB	0–4–0RT
Lyss, on display	8532 SBB	0–6–0T
Oberdorf, on display	11 SMB	2–8–0T
St. Gallen-Waldau, Playground	51 SOB	0–4–0T
Vallorbe, in store for *Verkehrshaus*	1367 SBB	2–6–0*
	705 SBB	4–6–0*
	35 JSB	4–4–0T*
	3 EB *Langnau*	0–6–0T*
	8512 SBB	0–6–0T*
	5819 SBB	2–6–2T*
	31 UeBB	Railcar*
	1 SCB *Gnom*	2–2–0RT*
	2 SCB *Elfe*	0–4–0RT*
Vitznau, Depot, SBB	16 RB	0–4–2RT*
	17 RB	0–4–2RT*
Wil, Depot MThB	3 MThB	2–6–2T*
	5810 MThB	2–6–2T*
Wildegg, Children's Playground	3 STB	0–6–0T
Winterthur, outside SLM Works	2969 SBB	2–10–0
Winterthur, Sulzer Bros., in service	5 HWB	0–6–0T
	2 RSG	2–6–0T
? for Technorama	1 SMB	2–6–0T
Zurich, SihlTB Depot	5 SihlTB	0–6–0T*
Privately preserved	8516 SBB	0–6–0T

Switzerland—Narrow Gauge

Location	Number	Type
Alpnachstad, Depot, PB	P-B 9	Railcar (rack)
	P-B 10	Railcar (rack)
Blonay Chamby	109	0–6–0T
Brig, Depot, FO	F-O 4	2–6–0T (r and a)
Capolago	FMG 2	0–4–2T (r and a)
Chur	VZ 6 *Breithorn*	0–4–2T (r and a)
Feldkirch, Austria	L-E-B 5	0–6–0T
Landquart, Depot, RhB	Rh-B 107	2–8–0
	Rh-B 11	2–6–0T
Liestal	W-B 5 *G. Thommen*	0–6–0T
Lucerne *Verkehrshaus der Schweiz*	SSB 18	0–6–0 Tram
	W-B 6 *Waldenburg*	0–6–0T
	1063	0–6–0T (r and a)
Les Brenets, Depot, R-D-B	R-d-B 2	0–6–0T*
Le Locle, Technical school	R-d-B 3	0–6–0T
Meiringen, privately preserved	208	2–6–0T
Meiringen, on display	1068	0–6–0T (r and a)

* *The locomotive is stored and, therefore, the location given is not permanent.*

Location	Number	Type
Samedan, Depot, RhB	Rh-B 108	2–8–0
	Rh-B 14	2–6–0T
Vallorbe Depot, SBB	R-d-B 1	0–6–0T*
	Rh-B 1 *Rhaetia*	2–6–0T*
Wil Modelleisen-bahnklub	FW 2 *Hornli*	0–6–0T
Winterthur Technorama	SSB 12	0–6–0 Tram
Zermatt, Depot, VZ	VZ 7 *Breithorn*	0–4–2T (r and a)

The locomotive is stored and, therefore, the location given is not permanent.

Appendix 3

Alterations and additions to December 31, 1970

ITALY   1435mm

FS 0–4–2T No 814.002 ex-Austrian Sudbahn Class 4 is being restored at the Leonardo da Vinci Museum in Milan.

FS 0–6–0T No 830.035. Other locomotives of the same Class are now out of use at Novi San Bovo Depot FS, and are no longer in use at Genoa Docks.

FS 0–6–0T No 851.036 is now preserved at Porto Gruaro on the Venice–Trieste line. In was built in 1905 by OM (works number 77) as *Rete Adriatica* No 2772, but was delivered to FS who had absorbed the *RA* in 1904.

FS 0–6–0T No 851.186 was built in 1909 by Saronno (works number 356). It is now displayed on a pedestal in the Public Garden at Como.
Sixty of these locomotives of Series 851 were built for *RA* 1898–1904 and these were followed by another one hiundred and forty-seven for FS. Similar locomotives were also built for the Siena Monte Antico Railway.

Sud Est 0–6–0T No 6 is now preserved at Bari Sud-Est Station. It was built in 1901 by St. Leonard (works number 1205).

950mm

2–6–0T No 43 of the *Ferrovie Complementari della Sardegna* has been restored and will be exhibited in Cagliari. It carries the works plates of SLM No 859 of 1894, but these originally belonged to No 45, a similar locomotive. The frames of No 43 are from No 5 built in 1887 by SLM (works number 488).

No R 301.2. Some of these locomotives were sent to Libya and Eritrea as being surplus to FS requirements.

0–4–4–0 Mallet four-cylinder compound Side Tank locomotive No 200 was built in 1909 for the *Ferrovie Complementari della Sardegna* by Schwartz-kopff (works number 4349). It has been restored for exhibition in Cagliari and is at present at Monserrato Pirri Depot FCS.

NETHERLANDS 750mm

0–6–0 Tram No 13 *SILVOLDE* of the *Geldersche Tramwegen* is now preserved at Doetinchem. It was built in 1900 by Backer and Rueb (works number 182).

NORWAY 1067mm

0–4–4T No 4 *HYGEIA* built in 1877 by Beyer Peacock is to be preserved at Stavanger Station. It worked on the Stavanger–Egersund line.

PORTUGAL

It now seems certain that a Railway Museum will be established at the site of the old locomotive depot at Entroncamento.

SPAIN 1674mm

0–6–0 No 030.2110. *PERRUCA* has probably been scrapped.

1000mm

0–6–0T No 103 *ORCANERA* came into the ownership of the Vascongados Railway which gave the engine its present name and number. It eventually went to the important mineral railway of the *Compania Minera de Sierre Menera*.

SWEDEN 1435mm

2–2–0T No 1 *LIMHAMN* was built in 1888 by Nydquist (works number 263) for the Malmo Limhamn Railway (MLJ). It was sold to the Kalmar Emmaboda Railway (KEJ) and in 1913 went to Vako Peat Moss in Smaland where it sank into the peat following an accident. It has now been recovered and will be preserved in the Malmo Technical Museum.

0–4–4T No 1229 Class W was built in 1914 by Nydquist (works number 1045) for SJ. It was one of five such locomotives and it is scheduled for preservation in the Railway Museum at Gävle.

o–6–oST No 3 *BERG* was built in 1907 by Nydquist (works number 860) for the Malmo Limhamn Railway (MLJ). It has been presented to the *Foreningen Skanska Jarnvagar* and is at present kept in the MLJ shed at Limhamn.

o–6–oT No 1112 Class K4 was built for SJ in 1911 by Atlas (works number 126). It was then Class Ke but was subsequently rebuilt as Class Kh (later Class K4). From 1936 to 1940 it worked on the Varberg Boras Herrljunga Railway (VBHJ) and is to go to the Vansbro Turist and Hembygdsforening.

2–6–2T No 1617 Class S6 was built in 1918 by Nydquist (works number 1130) for the Malmo Ystad Railway (MYJ). It was taken over by SJ in 1944 and will go to the Malmo Technical Museum.

2–6–4T No 1400 Class J was built in 1918 by Motala (works number 626) for SJ. It is to go to the Vansbro Turist and Hembygdsforening. Forty-five of the class were built for SJ between 1914 and 1918 and a further one was built in 1914 for the Ostra Skanes Railway as their No 21. It later became No 41 of the Kristinehamn Hassleholm Railway (CHJ) and in 1944 was taken over by SJ as their No 1652.

2–6–4T No 1344 Class J was built in 1917 by Motala (works number 610) for SJ and it will probably go to the Foreningen Skanska Railway for ultimate preservation.

Class J are inside cylinder 2–6–4 Side Tank locomotives with outside frames for the trailing bogie. They have Walschaerts valve gear, the return cranks and expansion links for which are outside.

o–8–oT No 576 SJ Class N has arrived at Gävle.

o–2–2 Steam Car built by Atlas in 1888 for the Hamlstad Nassjo Railway is now in the Railway Museum at Gävle.

o–2–2 Steam Car built by Oxelsund Flen Vastmanlands Railway (OFVJ) at Eskilstuna in 1884 (works number 2) for the Waxio Tingsryd Railway (WAJ) as their No 2. It is now in the Railway Museum at Gävle.

Steam Car of the Uddevalla Vanersborg Herrljunga Railway (UVHJ) is in the Railway Museum at Gävle.

891mm

o–6–oT No 7 *HAGFORS* was built in 1883 by Nydquist (works number 175) for the Nordmark Klarälvens Railway (NKLJ). It is now preserved at the Station at Hagfors.

2–8–oT No 3052 SJ Class N4p was built in 1939 by Motala (works number 868) for the Olands Railway (OJ) as their No 11. It went to SJ in 1947 and is now preserved at Bergsjo.

2–8–oT No 5 of the Ha Vallvik Railway built in 1917 by Nydquist (works number 1110) as Norra Ostergotland No 16. It went to SJ in 1950 becoming their No 3163 Class N6p. It is now preserved on the *Stockholm Roslagens Museiforening*.

Steam Railcar No 2 of the Nordmark Klarälvens Railway (NKlJ) is now preserved at Nordmark.

Steam Railcar *MAJORN* of the Dala Ockelbo Norrsundets Railway (DONJ) was built in 1888 by Atlas. It is now owned by Jarnvagarnas Museisallskap at Jadraas.

643mm

0–4–oT No 5 *KAROLINA* was built in 1919 by Orenstein (works number 7696) for a commercial firm, and in 1947 went to the Sodra Dalarnes Railway (SDJ). It is located in Stromsnasbruk for probable preservation.

0–8–oT No 1 *EDW. ENGESTROM* was built in 1884 by Delary (works number 1) for the Sodra Dalarnes Railway (SDJ). It is at Delary for preservation.

0–8–oT No 3 *AUGUST SCHMITZ* was built in 1887 by Delary (works number 4) for the Sodra Dalarnes Railway (SDJ). It is now located at Stromsnasbruk.

(The route of the SDJ was from Delary to Stromsnas, and it was operated by an industrial firm, Stromsnasbruk AB.)

600mm

0–8–oT No 2 was built in 1914 by Hartmann (works number 4183) for DFB as their No 2539. It was later sold to Emsfors as their No 2 and has now been acquired by a tourist railway running from Ahs to Bor (Ohs Bruks Jarnvag) near Varnamo in the south of Sweden. This Company also expect to acquire 0–8–oT No 1 *MORMOR* built in 1910 by Zobel (works number 119) for a private firm at Boda and which, since 1959, has been preserved in the Park at Nassjo.

SWITZERLAND

1000mm

0–4–0 Tram ex No 52 of Bern Tramways will probably go to Blonay Chamby Railway.

2–6–0T No 3 was built in 1913 by SLM (works number 2317) for the Furka Oberalp Railway. It is now located at Hamby and will go to the Blonay Chamby Railway.

BIBLIOGRAPHY

During the compilation of this book I have made great use of the books in my library. Those which have been most frequently consulted are given below:

Articulated Locomotives—Wiener
Century of Locomotive Building—Warren
Concise Encyclopedia of World Railway Locomotives—Ed. P. Ransome-Wallis
Der Dampfbetrieb der Schweizerischen Eisenbahn—Moser
Dampflokomotiven—Holzborn
Deutschlands Dampflokomotiven—Maedel
Driftsmaterial I—DSB
Engins Moteurs—SNCF
Geschichte der italienischen Dampflokomotiven—Messerschmidt
Nos Inoubliables "Vapeur"—Dambly
Last Steam Locomotives of Western Europe—Ransome-Wallis
Locomotives of the Danish State Railways—Bay
Locomotives of the Private Railways of Denmark—Bay
Locomotives à Vapeur Françaises—Vilain
Le Matériel Moteurs de la SNCF—Defrance
Nordens Järnvagar
Onze Nederlands Locomotieven—Waldorp
Railway Holiday in Bavaria—Price
Un Siècle de Matériel et Traction sur le Reseau d'Orléans—Vilain
Steam on the RENFE—Marshall
Verzeichnis der Deutschen Lokomotiven, 1923–65—Schadow
World's Locomotives—Lake

The Locomotive—Volumes I–65
The Railway Engineer—various volumes
The Railway Gazette—various volumes
Railway Scene—several issues
Le Vie du Rail—various volumes